UNLOCKING THE POWER OF COMMERCIAL REIT INVESTING

A COMPREHENSIVE GUIDE TO LOW-RISK REIT INVESTING FOR PASSIVE INCOME, STABILITY, AND FINANCIAL FREEDOM

MILES BIRD

TABLE OF CONTENTS

PART THREE
REAL STORIES AND STRATEGIES

INTRODUCTION

I have navigated the intricate construction of real estate for over two decades. The essence of this book is not just my passion for real estate but my sheer fascination with the empowerment Commercial REITs offer to everyday investors. Whether you are an interested beginner, an intermediate strategist, or a seasoned pro, this guide promises to illuminate your path, at the very least. The key takeaways for anyone starting on this journey are essential. While REITs offer a taste of the real estate market's riches, they are not all crafted from the same mold. Some directly invest in properties, bathing in the steady glow of rental income and management fees. Others delve into the world of real estate debt, exploring mortgages and their accompanying securities, and each REIT often echoes a particular song–the bustling energy of shopping centers, the serene ambiance of healthcare facilities, or the dynamic pulse of hotels and resorts (Ashworth, 2023).

The allure of the real estate market has always been significant, promising lucrative returns and stability in turbulent times. Real estate investment trusts (REITs) have emerged as an essential tool in an investor's arsenal, bridging the vast world of real estate and the average investor. When smartly integrated into an equity or fixed-income portfolio, REITs offer a delightful blend of diversification, promising returns, and a buffer against the volatile dance of stocks, bonds, and cash (Ashworth, 2023).

REITs serve as a golden ticket for individuals to plunge into the world of expansive, revenue-generating properties. Think of a REIT as a powerhouse entity, owning and usually managing assets that churn out income, like majestic office towers, busy shopping arcades, cozy apartments, luxury hotels, and even spaces like self-storage units or sprawling warehouses. Here is a distinction: A REIT is in it for the long game, unlike the typical real estate firms that create properties only to flip them. They are the grand strategists, purchasing and sculpting properties to weave them seamlessly into their esteemed investment construction (Investor.gov, n.d.).

Looking into the world of Non-Traded REITs (A non-traded REIT refers to REITs that are not listed but traded on a public exchange), or those not tied to stock exchanges, introduces investors to a unique set of challenges. Since these REITs are not in the public domain, researching them is akin to navigating a maze without a map. Consequently, pinpointing the exact value of your investment is a tough nut to crack. True, some non-traded REITs may lift the veil on assets and values around the 18-month mark, but that is hardly a silver lining. Their illiquidity is another stumbling block. Sometimes, the market lacks buyers or sellers just when you're itching to make a move. Selling these REITs is often off the table for a long stretch–think seven years.

A few might let you cash out a slice after a year, but that is often with a catch: a fee. Their modus operandi revolves around pooling funds to acquire and oversee properties. But here is the twist: sometimes, dividends are rolled out from other investors' pockets rather than from property-generated income. This tactic restricts the REIT's cash flow and trims down share value. Upfront fees? They are quite the pinch! Most non-traded REITs dip into your pocket, taking away anywhere between 9% to 15%. While some of these REITs might boast impeccable management and prime real estate, it is essential to remember that publicly traded REITs can offer similar perks without many of the associated risks. External manager fees can further gnaw at your returns. If you are venturing into this territory, grill the management. Seek clarity.

Remember, transparency is gold. Publicly traded REITs are often considered the safer bet, weaving real estate into your investment narrative while serving up enticing dividends. But they are not without pitfalls. The looming shadow of rising interest rates can cool off the REIT fervor. As rates climb, many investors cozy up to more secure income avenues like U.S. Treasuries, making REITs less appealing. However, silver linings exist–a booming economy often accompanies rising rates, hinting at higher rents and entire proper-ties. Yet, historically, REITs and surging interest rates are not the best of pals. Selecting the right REIT is both an art and a science. It is about using logic and foresight. Case in point: the waning appeal of suburban malls. Is investing in a REIT that primarily invests in suburban malls wise? Your best bet would be no. Metropolitan shop-ping hubs might be your winning ticket with the modern shift towards urban settings. It might not scream "risk," but the tax implica-tions can weigh heavily on some investors. REIT dividends get taxed as regular income. In layman's terms, you are probably paying more than you would for dividend taxes or stock capital gains (Moskowitz, 2022).

However, REITs are not a one-size-fits-all affair. Their spectrum is diverse, with each type of REIT bearing its unique characteristics, rewards, and risks. At their core, REITs own and/or manage income-producing commercial real estate. This might be in the form of the properties themselves or the mortgages tethered to these properties. As an investor, you are presented with multiple avenues to dive into the REIT world– individually, through exchange-traded funds, or mutually funded and these options, the landscape is dotted with various types of REITs, each echoing the heartbeats of different sectors of the property market (Ashworth, 2023). Yet, one category often goes unnoticed among the myriad REIT types available:

Government REITs. Tucked away like the most precious gem in our treasure chest, Government REITs represent a fusion of stability, given their association with government entities and the inherent advantages of REIT investments.

One undeniable charm of REITs is their commitment to rewarding their shareholders. Bound by regulations, they are mandated to return 90% of taxable income to those who invest in them, manifesting as high-yield dividends. It is a commitment few other investment avenues can boast. However, remember that our treasure chest's gleaming coins are not all gold. Some might be silver, and others might be bronze.

Similarly, REIT dividends have their tax implications, a slight hiccup in an otherwise promising journey. Historically, the trajectory of REITs has been an upward climb. They showcased enviable returns when pitted against the U.S. real estate market benchmarks, like the FTSE NAREIT Equity REIT Index. Over lengthy periods, they have outshined stalwarts like the S&P 500, underscoring the wisdom of including them in a diverse portfolio. Embrace this unique REIT approach, paying attention to every nook and cranny, especially the often-underestimated Government REITs.

Your map is in your hands; the treasure awaits. Let the journey begin with a mental journey. Picture yourself in the heart of a large/major City, standing before a towering skyscraper–one that touches the edges of the sky. The reflections of taxis and pedestrians shimmer on its gleaming glass surface. Now, imagine if you had a stake in that building. Or how about owning a piece of a busy shopping mall in Paris or a prime office space in Tokyo? Sounds like a dream, right? But there is a twist. You do not need millions in the bank to make this dream come true. I invite you to the incredible world of commercial REITs! With the proper knowledge, anyone can unlock the bounty inside, reaping the dual rewards of capital appreciation and regular income.

As we journey on this expedition, exploring the world of Commercial REIT Investing, let us channel our inner explorers, armed with the knowledge and strategies laid out in the ensuing chapters. For in this quest, the treasure is real, and the rewards are tangible. Your map is in your hands; the bounty awaits. Let the journey begin.

PART ONE
UNDERSTANDING COMMERCIAL REITS

CHAPTER 1
THE PATH TO FINANCIAL INDEPENDENC

IN A BUSY URBAN LANDSCAPE, picture two individuals: Emily, a traditional real estate investor, and David, an enthusiast of the stock market. Both have dreams as tall as skyscrapers, hoping to build wealth and achieve financial independence. Emily's journey involves dealing with brokers, handling property maintenance, and navigating tenant relations. On the other hand, David is glued to stock tickers, diligently tracking market fluctuations and reading company reports. Their paths seem divergent, each fraught with its unique challenges and rewards. What if there was a middle ground? A way that combined the tangible assets of Emily's real estate with the liquidity and ease of David's stocks. This is the world of Commercial REITs

Commercial REITs offer a fascinating blend of real estate and stock market investments. They provide the opportunity to own a slice of prime real estate properties without the direct hassles of property management. Simultaneously, like stocks, they can be bought or sold on major securities exchanges, offering liquidity and flexibility. For individuals like Emily and David, REITs can serve as a bridge, harnessing the strengths of both worlds. Instead of dealing with midnight plumbing emergencies or the volatility of individual stocks, they can invest in a portfolio of income-generating properties. This not only offers the potential for regular dividends but also the possibility of capital appreciation in the long run. But it is not just about the low-risk Passive Income (ROI). Commercial REITs play a significant role in community development, transforming skylines and contributing to local economies. For an investor, this means being a part of something bigger–contributing to societal growth while also working towards personal financial independence (Batt et al., 2022).

PART I: UNDERSTANDING COMMERCIAL REITS

A BRIEF HISTORY OF REITS

REITs have bridged the gap between real estate and stock investments. The inception of REITs in the United States was a pivotal moment in financial history, driven by a legislative vision in 1960. This vision sought to democratize the realm of income-producing real estate, allowing access not just to the wealthy elite but to all, especially the small investor. President Dwight D. Eisenhower, recognizing the transformative potential of REITs, signed legislation in 1960. This historic act fused the best attributes of real estate and stock-based investments, allowing everyday Americans to partake in the benefits of commercial real estate investments. Before this, these perks were exclusive to large financial institutions or affluent individuals. Returning to the 1960s, REITs underwent a significant transformation with the Tax Reform Act of 1986. This reform empowered REITs to not only own but also operate and manage real estate. Through the years, the essence of REITs has remained intact–an inclusive investment model aiming to offer all Americans a slice of the commercial real estate pie. Today, nearly 45% of American households, which translates to about 150 million citizens, have a stake in REITs directly or through financial instruments like mutual funds, ETFs, or target date funds (Nareit, n.d.)

The reach of REITs is not confined to the U.S. Inspired by the success of the U.S. model, around 40 countries, encompassing all G-7 nations and a significant fraction of OECD countries, have integrated the REIT framework, granting investors worldwide access to rich portfolios of income-generating real estate. So, what exactly is a REIT? At its core, a REIT is a corporate entity that owns, operates, or finances properties that produce income. It is a unique fusion, mirroring mutual funds, where the capital of countless investors is amalgamated. This system allows individual investors to reap dividends from real estate endeavors without the hassles of buying, managing, or financing properties themselves.

To delve deeper, the origins of REITs trace back to a pivotal moment in 1960 when Congress, through the Cigar Excise Tax Extension, allowed investors to invest in commercial real estate portfolios. This innovative approach to real estate introduced an array of property types to potential investors, from apartment complexes and data centers to hotels and office buildings. Furthermore, REITs are known for their specificity; they typically specialize in distinct real estate sectors. However, diversified and specialty REITs also hold a mix of property types. Many of these REITs trade on major securities exchanges, and like stocks, they are liquid and accessible to investors.

Origins and Aims of REITs

Designed to function as mutual funds for commercial real estate, the initial purpose behind REITs was to democratize investment in this sector. By offering a way to invest without the typical liquidity challenges or significant capital outlays, REITs cater to the average individual. These trusts became accessible through direct stock market transactions and various retirement and investment funds. Thanks to their hybrid nature, blending elements of stocks and bonds, REITs delivered consistent dividends, acted as a diversifying factor in portfolios, and drew a vast pool of about 145 million American investors by 2020 (Batt et al., 2022).

Regulations and Requirements

The IRS outlines specific guidelines that REITs must adhere to. Beyond the core provisions like having 75% of assets in real estate, deriving 75% of gross income from real property, and distributing at least 90% of dividends, REITs are expected to draw at most 5% of their income from non-real estate sources. Structurally, they should have a board of directors, transferable shares, a minimum of 100 shareholders after their first year, and restrict five or fewer individuals from holding over 50% of their shares.

Evolution and Adaptations

The continuous advocacy efforts of the real estate sector have tailored REIT regulations over the years, making them more investor-friendly and closely aligned with traditional corporate property ownership while retaining their tax benefits. Multiple administrations, spanning both political parties, have made amendments to the original 1960 law. Notably, the Tax Reform Act of 1986 permitted REITs to manage their properties directly and even engage in service provision, moving away from their initial passive investment role. Subsequent reforms like the REIT Modernization Act of 1999 and the REIT Investment and Diversification Act of 2008 further expanded REIT functionalities and operational capacities. These changes have made it easier for them to purchase assets, capture more rental revenue, and allow specific sectors, like healthcare REITs, to enjoy benefits similar to hotel REITs. Additionally, the 2015 PATH Act and the 2017 Tax Cuts and Jobs Act provided more favorable tax provisions, strengthening REITs' appeal to domestic and foreign investors.

Growth Trajectory of REITs

Post their inception, REITs experienced modest growth until the 1990s. However, the financial landscape of the 90s, characterized by drying traditional real estate financing and a national recession, paved the way for REITs to flourish. Institutional investors began seeing them as a liquid alternative to direct real estate investments. From being a minor player in the 1990s, REITs started accounting for a significant portion of equity financing by the early 2000s. This growth trajectory is evident in the rise of the total number of REITs from 46 in 1975 to a staggering 223 by 2020.

Features of REITs

REITs can be broadly divided into three main categories: Equity REITs, Mortgage REITs, and Hybrid REITs. Equity REITs are primarily concerned with owning and managing real estate assets, whereas Mortgage REITs are centered on investing in mortgages. Hybrid REITs, on the other hand, employ the investment strategies of both equity and mortgage REITs, giving them a unique position in the market.

According to a study by Batt et al. (2022), while Mortgage REITs, commonly termed mREITs, predominantly cater to the housing sector, Equity REITs hold a commanding presence in the market, accounting for approximately 82%, a statistic corroborated by Krewson-Kelly and Thomas in 2016. On the other hand, Hybrid REITs deftly merge the strategies of both Equity and Mortgage REITs, carving out their unique niche in this investment ecosystem.

Historically, until around 2010, the REIT domain was dominated by conventional commercial real estate segments such as apartments, office spaces, warehouses, and shopping centers. However, the landscape began to shift with the advent of 'non-traditional REITs (A non-traditional REIT refers to REITs that are not listed but traded on a public exchange), with sectors like healthcare and hotels gaining traction. Notably, a vast majority of REITs specialize in specific sectors. A mere fraction (less than 20 out of over 220) of publicly traded REITs spread their investments across multiple industries. But, even within their chosen sectors, REITs often diversify by investing in various brands or operational entities.

For equity REITs in sectors like healthcare and hotels, 'triple net leases (N) have become prevalent. These expenses are in addition to the cost of rent. In contrast, in standard commercial lease agreements, some or all of these payments are typically the landlord's responsibility. NNNs are just one type of commercial property net lease. A single net lease requires tenants to pay property taxes and rent; a double net lease typically tacks on property insurance.

Furthermore, they promise reduced volatility and tend to fare better during economic downturns. For instance, during the Great Recession, healthcare REITs, NNN, suffered the least setbacks among all sectors. REITs that favor these leases typically pursue growth through acquisitions, necessitating them to ensure their capital costs remain competitive. With interest rates consistently low since the Great Recession, triple net leases are competitive and lucrative to REIT investors. With the U.S. Federal Reserve Bank initiating a rise in interest rates to counteract inflationary pressures, a silver lining emerges for discerning commercial REIT investors. This shift paves the way for those keen on NNN and other opportunities arising from the reduction in competitive intensity. By being well-informed, proactive, and astutely reading the nuances of the commercial REIT market, you will find solace in knowing your decisions are grounded in low-risk strategies yet positioned for high rewards. For this reason, this book is also crafted to arm you with the knowledge, foresight, and assurance required to thrive in Commercial REIT investing.

LANDLORD VS. REITS (ADVANTAGES AND DRAWBACKS)

An interesting article by Depersio (2021) enlightens us on the differences between Landlord and REITS.

Advantages of Being a Landlord

Owning rental property offers a notable advantage: leverage. With a strong credit score, investors can acquire a rental asset by paying just 20% upfront and mortgaging the rest. For instance, for a $100,000 property, an investor might only need an initial investment of $20,000. If the property's value rises by 20% within the first year—a plausible scenario in a booming market—the investor could see a 100% return on investment. Even with mortgage obligations, astute investors can garner sufficient rental income to cover all costs and make a profit. This dual revenue stream, from both property value appreciation and tenant rents, is appealing.

Drawbacks of Being a Landlord

Owning rental properties demands hands-on management versus investing in REITs. Many landlords find managing their assets as time-consuming as a full-time occupation. Those considering this path should anticipate a significant time investment or be ready to hire a professional manager to oversee details, from promoting vacancies to handling rent collection and problematic tenants. Furthermore, property ownership comes with its fair share of costs. Based on the lease terms, landlords could bear financial responsibility for a wide range of maintenance issues. These unexpected expenses can quickly diminish a landlord's ROI. Plus, addressing emergency maintenance issues, like plumbing problems, can disrupt personal life.

Pros of REIT Investment

The prime attraction of REITs is their simplicity. They allow investors to benefit from property appreciation and rental revenue without the direct challenges of property ownership. Additionally, REITs present an opportunity for diversification. While building a varied portfolio through direct property purchases demands a significant budget, time, and know-how, a carefully chosen REIT provides diversity in a single, straightforward transaction. It is also noteworthy that, unlike direct property investments, which can be challenging to liquidate, especially in a sluggish market, REIT shares can be easily converted to cash, often with just a quick phone call.

Cons of REIT Investment

Unlike direct property ownership, REITs do not offer the leverage benefits derived from property financing. Given the legal requirement for REITs to distribute 90% of their earnings to shareholders, only 10% remains for reinvestment in new assets. As a result, REIT shares may be less volatile, especially compared to high-growth sectors like tech, which is a volatile sector. Another consideration is the need for direct control of REIT investments. While property owners can personally inspect and research their potential assets, REIT investors must trust others with these decisions. This indirect approach can be perfect for some, but those who lean towards a more hands-on strategy might find direct property ownership more appealing.

Influence of Macroeconomic Risks on Property-specific REITs

This research study by Patterson (2009) delves deep into how broader economic risk factors affect REITs specializing in specific property types across various economic sectors. While numerous studies have examined how economic risks impact Equity REITs, they typically viewed REITs as one homogenous group.

However, this study's results present a different narrative. The influence of economic risks on REIT returns varies significantly depending on the type of property they invest in. In other words, a REIT focusing on commercial properties might respond differently to economic changes compared to one centered around residential properties.

Moreover, the study observed that these property-specific REITs also show different reactions when faced with unexpected events or 'information shocks' stemming from alterations in economic conditions. The size of the REIT–whether it is a large, medium, or small enterprise–further compounds these differences. This size factor plays a dual role, affecting the overall sensitivity to economic changes and how REITs respond dynamically as these changes unfold.

In essence, this research sheds light on the nuanced relationship between macroeconomic risks and REIT returns, depending on property types and the size of the trusts. Such insights are invaluable for investors, helping shape more informed portfolio-building strategies and managing risk in the real estate investment landscape.

The Impact of Rising Interest Rates on REITs

Over the last quarter-century, REITs have become a favored method for investors of varying profiles to tap into the real estate market. They offer impressive long-term returns, liquidity, high dividend yields, and diversification potential, making them especially attractive. Nevertheless, there are rising apprehensions about the performance of REITs as interest rates surge. Data from S&P Dow Jones Indices and Barclays Capital between May 1992 and May 2017 illustrates that REITs have typically outperformed major asset classes like stocks, bonds, and commodities (Orzano & Welling, 2017).

It is widely believed that REITs will underperform in an environment with a rising interest rate. However, historical data challenges this idea. While higher interest rates undeniably influence real estate values and REIT performance, a direct correlation between rising rates and negative returns does not exist. Over the past decades, there have been six instances where 10-year U.S. Treasury Bond yields surged substantially. Remarkably, REITs produced positive returns in four of these six instances.

Moreover, in half of these occasions, they outperformed the S&P 500. Rising interest rates do present hurdles for REITs. They can diminish property values, elevate borrowing costs, and make the dividends from REITs less attractive when mixed with fixed-income securities. However, such rates are often tied to positive economic indicators like growth and inflation, which can buoy real estate investments. A booming economy typically means more demand for real estate, boosting REIT earnings, cash flow, and dividends. During inflationary times, landlords often raise rents, and historically, REIT dividend growth has surpassed inflation rates.

Warren Buffett once said, "It is wise for investors to be fearful when others are greedy and to be greedy only when others are fearful." (Brownlee, 2023, p. 1). This perspective goes against the grain of conventional stock market thinking, tying directly to an asset's price. When the masses get greedy, prices tend to skyrocket, warranting caution to avoid overpaying and subsequently earning lackluster returns. However, when fear is in the air, it might just be the right time for savvy value investment.

The direction of interest rate movements is not the sole determinant of REITs' performance. The underlying economic reasons for rate changes, particularly economic strength and inflation, can have more profound implications for REITs. These factors can counterbalance the potential negative impacts of increasing rates. From the perspective of an informed REIT investor, consider this example: A REIT that is not performing well might offer a prime investment entry point. Situations like inflation and escalating interest rates can have severe repercussions for landlords. These increasing rates can swiftly transform a profitable property into a financial burden. To cope, commercial property landlords might hike prices, potentially driving away tenants and adversely affecting their Debt Service Coverage Ratio. Most seasoned investors would advise patience during periods of increasing interest rates, waiting for the situation to stabilize. In such circumstances, the data suggests that it might be wiser for a REIT investor to hold off and be ready to act when conditions appear more favorable. For astute REIT investing, understanding these dynamics is crucial. With this foundational knowledge, a REIT investor can approach the market with greater confidence and have a broader range of strategies to optimize both short-term and long-term returns.

OFF TO A GOOD START

We started this chapter by painting a picture of the bustling urban environment; two individuals emerge. Emily is a traditional real estate enthusiast, and David is a stock market aficionado. Both harbor dreams of wealth and financial autonomy. Emily's path is filled with brokers, property issues, and tenant interactions, while David is engrossed in stock market dynamics. However, Commercial REITs offer a bridge between these two realms, merging real estate's tangibility with the fluidity of stocks.

Commercial REITs, a blend of real estate and stocks, allow investors to partake in the benefits of property ownership without the associated hassles. These trusts are liquid, traded on major exchanges, and present a portfolio of income-generating properties. Beyond financial gains, they significantly impact community development. When they discussed the concept of REITs in 1960, the U.S. aimed to democratize commercial real estate investments. This vision transformed real estate investment, making it accessible to the masses, not just the elite. Over time, REITs expanded globally, with around 40 countries adopting the framework. Essentially, REITs consolidate investor capital, allowing individuals to benefit from real estate ventures without directly managing properties.

Comparing direct property ownership with REITs, being a landlord offers leverage benefits and the potential for high returns. However, it demands significant hands-on management. Conversely, REITs offer simplicity, diversification, and liquidity but may need more rapid growth of direct real estate due to distribution requirements.

In this chapter, you dove deep into the world of Commercial REITs, elucidating their history, evolution, advantages, and the broader ecosystem that supports and regulates them. Thus, in the next chapter, you may question what lies at the heart of this enigmatic blend. As we pull back the curtains, we unveil the world of Commercial REITs, a bridge that merges the tangibility of skyscrapers with the fluidity of stock tickers. Dive deeper with me as we journey through the evolution and nuances of this fascinating investment avenue, demystifying its complexities and revealing its true potential.

CHAPTER 2

DEMYSTIFYING COMMERCIAL REIT

The Enigma of Real Estate Trusts

WITHIN THE CAPTIVATING realm of Real Estate Trusts, many associate the ownership of gleaming skyscrapers, bustling malls, and expansive office spaces with magnates and property moguls; the truth reveals a different narrative. Many of the international iconic properties are actually governed by entities listed in the diversified REIT sector on stock exchanges. These entities collectively control an overwhelming portion of global urban and industrial landscapes.

Unveiling the Building Blocks of Commercial REITs

The Commercial REITs sector evolved from property unit trusts and property loan stock companies to embrace the unique tax structure offered by REITs, allowing earnings to flow through to investors without a company-level income tax. Despite the tax benefits, investors in REIT shares are not immune to capital gains tax. While major players like Growthpoint Properties and Redefine Properties dominate with billions in assets, the sector faces challenges from pandemic-induced remote working, impacting office rentals and mall lease renewals. Notable entities diversify portfolios, with challenges including economic struggles, inflation, and infrastructural issues. Smaller players like Fortress Real Estate Investment and Investec Property Fund add complexity with unique offerings, and the sector's future hinges on factors like the return to office spaces and the potential repurposing of shopping areas. Savvy investors are anticipating opportunities amid growing apprehensions about the stock market.

Section 2: Advantages of REITs

As expressed before, REITs stand as a bridge between the world of commercial real estate and publicly traded stocks, offering investors the best of both worlds. They combine the lucrative attributes of property investment with the dynamic nature of stock market trading. Historically, the performance of income-driven real estate has blessed REIT investors with competitive, long-standing returns, balancing out the gains from other stock investments and bonds.

A pivotal characteristic of REITs is their mandate to disburse at least 90% of their taxable earnings to shareholders yearly through dividends. This percentage, noticeably higher than many other equity classes, has consistently delivered a robust income stream, weathering diverse market climates.

REITs stand out for their historical performance and potential for diversifying portfolios and come with unique perks seldom seen in other industry sectors. This suite of advantages has escalated the popularity of REITs among investors over successive decades.

A significant chunk of a REIT's dependable income emanates from rents gathered from commercial properties. These properties are often tied up in long-term lease agreements or stem from interest accrued from financing said properties. At their core, most REITs embrace a lucid, intuitive business paradigm. They lease out spaces, amass rents from their real estate portfolio, and subsequently channel this income to shareholders as dividends. Like other public enterprises, REITs must disclose their financial performance, presenting earnings per share rooted in the net income metrics dictated by Generally Accepted Accounting Principles (GAAP) (Nareit, n.d.-b).

Section 3: Debunking Myths on REITS

The realm of commercial real estate investment beckons with its promises of lucrative gains. However, common misconceptions often deter potential investors from embarking on this rewarding journey. This article by Summerhill Commercial (2023) aims to address and debunk some of these myths to provide a clearer picture.

- Myth #1: High Capital is Mandatory for Commercial Real Estate Investment.

While making a more substantial financial commitment can sometimes yield more significant returns, the commercial real estate sector offers various entry points suitable for different investment capacities. For instance, REITs provide an avenue for investors to own a slice of a diversified property portfolio without the hands-on hassle. Furthermore, pooling resources with other investors or joining a syndicate extends the possibility of venturing into more prominent, potentially more lucrative deals than relying on solo capital.

- Myth #2: Commercial Real Estate is a High-Risk Endeavour

Like all investments, commercial real estate comes with its risks. However, the risk factor is not inherently high. One can navigate toward low-risk, high-reward opportunities with proper research, due diligence, and well-informed decisions. A savvy investor will always have a financial safety net, ensuring they are prepared for unforeseen expenses or vacancies, thus avoiding potential pitfalls.

- Myth #3: Prior Experience in Commercial Real Estate is Essential.

Indeed, a seasoned background in commercial real estate gives one an edge. However, it is optional for achieving success in this domain. Today, budding investors can access abundant online resources, from informative blogs to insightful podcasts, which can lay down the foundational knowledge. Moreover, collaborating with seasoned mentors or professionals can fast-track one's learning curve, and this advice and guidance can be both impactful and cost-effective.

The allure of commercial real estate investment is undeniable, offering opportunities for sustained, long-term gains. It is essential to understand that these common myths should not deter potential investors. Instead, with diligent research, continuous education, and guidance from industry experts, one can navigate this realm confidently, irrespective of their prior experience or financial standing. Ultimately, the commercial real estate landscape is open for all, ready to reward those who approach it with the right mix of caution, knowledge, and enthusiasm.

Section 4: Examining the Legal Frameworks of REITs

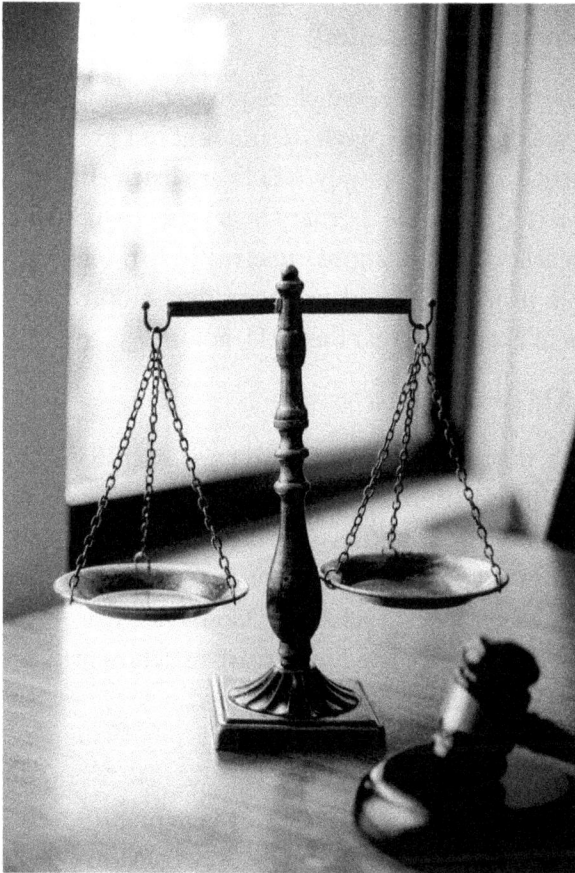

Countries worldwide have been instituting frameworks allowing investors to invest in real estate via capital markets, regardless of their financial size. These are recognized as Real Estate Investment Trusts or REITs. The laws governing these trusts differ based on the country, but all operate under the principle that most yearly profits are distributed as dividends to the shareholders. In its 2019 Budget speech, Malta revealed its intention to set up a REITs framework to trade on the Malta Stock Exchange (MSE). This new asset class aims to generate rental income, granting opportunities to investors who might be unable to invest in the local property market directly. Introducing REITs is also anticipated to infuse more liquidity into the property sector.

REITs vs. Property Companies

Unlike property companies, which acquire real estate to develop and sell, REITs are designed to purchase and rent out properties as part of an investment strategy. Typically, REITs are listed entities with shares that can be traded in the primary markets. To mitigate risks and potential market manipulations, many REIT frameworks mandate that a single property should not represent more than 40% of the entire value of properties that the REIT holds.

Universal REIT Features

Even though there are unique features for each REIT based on its location and jurisdiction, there are some shared characteristics. For instance, while some countries like the U.S. and Japan allow varied legal structures for REITs, others like Singapore offer tax incentives for those listed on stock exchanges. Countries like Australia, Hong Kong, and Mexico typically adopt a trust structure, while nations like Canada prefer mutual fund trust structures.

REITs in Malta

Looking further into our initial case of Malta in 2019, while they have needed to catch up in adopting REITs, they recognize the potential of strategically leveraging and modeling Its framework after the successful examples from countries like the U.S., U.K., and Hong Kong. Malta is leaning towards the model of a listed Public Limited Company (PLC), a corporate entity overseen by directors and owned by shareholders. This kind of company can make its shares available to the general public. It is a limited liability company with shares that the public can easily buy and sell—a structure influenced by the U.K.'s approach, which has significantly impacted Malta's corporate law. If adopted, these public companies must be tax residents in Malta and can be structured through the appropriate authority. A mandate requiring REITs to list a portion of their shares on the MSE would enhance investor protection due to listing transparency and foster participation from a broader range of investors (Parker, 2019).

Associations Related to REITs

Imagine walking through the vast financial districts of a large metropolis. There are impressive skyscrapers housing world-renowned corporations that also stand as a testament to the vast potential of real estate as an investment avenue. For the individual investor, diving into such waters might seem daunting, but with the help of various associations and government bodies, the landscape is made more accessible. Below are several U.S. and international associations and organizations centered on REITs provided by The Law Library of Congress (n.d.).

- National Association of Real Estate Investment Trusts (NAREIT)

NAREIT is a representative body for REITs and publicly traded real estate entities focusing on real estate and capital markets. Its website offers educational content, datasets, REIT assets, and investment fund details. Let us consider Jane, a young professional interested in dipping her toes into the world of real estate investments. She stumbled upon NAREIT while researching and found it a treasure trove. NAREIT sheds light on the workings of REITs and gives her insights into real estate's nuances and the capital market's dynamics.

- Real Estate Research Institute (RERI)

Established in 1987, RERI is a charitable entity encouraging research into real estate investment performance and fundamental market knowledge, especially concerning private equity REITs. Picture Tom, a research student aiming to draw parallels between historical real estate performance and future projections. RERI becomes his academic ally, opening up avenues of well-researched data and studies about the transformative role of private equity REITs over the years.

- Government Resources on REITs

REITs are subject to comprehensive local, state, and federal regulation. Hence, resources from governmental agencies can augment your understanding of each government REIT asset class.

- Fannie Mae (Federal National Mortgage Association)

A U.S. government-backed entity and a publicly listed company, Fannie Mae provides

- industry updates,
- pricing details for mortgage-backed securities and debt instruments, and
- a marketplace for homes owned by Fannie Mae.
- Freddie Mac (Federal Home Loan Mortgage Corporation)

Congressionally chartered and a public government-sponsored entity, Freddie Mac is pivotal in amplifying funds availability to mortgage lenders via mortgage purchases, guarantees, and securitization. The platform offers consumer insights on home investment and facilitates loan generation.

- Federal Reserve Board

Engaged in comprehensive research, the Federal Reserve Board produces papers, statistics, and reports on various financial and economic aspects, including details on real estate finance, mortgages, and related securities.

- Ginnie Mae (Government National Mortgage Association)

Established in 1968, Ginnie Mae, a Department of Housing and Urban Development (HUD) division, focuses on expanding affordable housing finance in the U.S. This entity guarantees mortgages in secondary markets and offers resources for potential homeowners.

- U.S. Securities and Exchange Commission (SEC)

REITs enable individual investments in large-scale, revenue-generating real estate supervised by the SEC. The SEC's platform offers a comprehensive REIT overview, including investor alerts and bulletins.

- European Public Real Estate Association (EPRA)

EPRA represents Europe's publicly listed property sector, shifting the focus to a more international realm. They provide indices, research data, and comprehensive guides on European REITs.

- Asia Pacific Real Estate Association (APREA)

APREA offers various resources, research, and networking opportunities for those interested in the Asia-Pacific region's vibrant real estate market. Investment Property Forum (IPF).

- Operating in the U.K., the IPF endeavors to enhance the understanding and efficiency of commercial property as an investment medium.

SECTION 5: RECENT TRENDS IN REITS

Recently, REITs have emerged as pivotal players within the vast investment playground. As avenues that grant access to real estate assets without needing direct property ownership, REITs represent an innovative blend of stability and profitability (as mentioned earlier). Their appeal stems not just from the tangible assets they represent but also from the fluidity and diversity they introduce to an investment portfolio. The breadth and depth of the REIT industry are truly remarkable. Recent statistics reveal that REITs command over $4.5 trillion in real estate assets, encompassing a staggering 535,000 properties. The physical assets under REITs' purview have reshaped urban landscapes, from metropolitan skyscrapers to expansive malls and cozy apartments. But the value is not just in brick and mortar. By the end of 2021, REITs had infused a whopping $92.3 billion back into the economy via dividends, underpinning over 3 million jobs simultaneously. Such figures reinforce the economic significance of REITs, painting them as more than mere investment vehicles.

Historical data provides another layer to the REIT narrative. Over the years, these entities have consistently offered competitive returns to their investors, a feat achieved through a combination of regular dividends and long-term capital appreciation. The growth trajectory of REITs regarding listings and market capitalization signals their ever-increasing gravitas in the real estate capital markets. Their growth is not just confined to the U.S.; the global adoption of the REIT model speaks volumes about its success and sustainability.

However, like all investment avenues, REITs are not without their nuances. Proper valuation remains crucial. Therefore, it is imperative to recognize the intricacies inherent in this investment avenue. Effective valuation is paramount, and investors often concentrate on key indicators such as the Price-to-Funds From Operations (P/FFO) and Net Asset Value (NAV) premiums/discounts.

1. Price-to-FFO Ratio:

- *Significance:* Evaluate the market's assessment of a REIT's cash-generating capabilities.
- *Example:* A low P/FFO ratio may indicate undervaluation, prompting investor interest.

2. NAV Premiums/Discounts:

- *Significance:* Reflects the market's perception of a REIT's asset portfolio and future cash flows.
- *Example:* REITs often trading at NAV discounts might attract investors seeking potential undervalued assets.

Understanding these indicators empowers investors to gauge whether REIT shares align appropriately with the intrinsic value of underlying assets and anticipated cash flows. The observation that REITs commonly trade at NAV discounts adds a layer of complexity, inviting investors to explore unique market perceptions and potential strategic investment opportunities. In other words, these help investors discern whether REIT shares are priced aptly in relation to the intrinsic value of their asset portfolios and projected cash flows. For instance, the observed trend wherein REITs trade at NAV discounts offers a fascinating insight into market perceptions and potential investment strategies.

The future landscape of REITs, as sketched by financial think tanks and analysts, is intriguing. Fitch, a globally recognized credit rating agency, has revised its 2023 outlook for U.S. REITs to "Deteriorating" from a previously neutral stance. This shift underscores potential challenges, from stricter commercial real estate lending parameters to headwinds from increasing interest rates. Yet, the silver lining remains.

The global REIT market is poised to expand at a Compound Annual Growth Rate (CAGR) of 2.8% from 2022 to 2027, potentially adding a substantial $333 billion in value. This growth, coupled with several countries' adoption of the U.S. REIT model, ensures that REITs remain at the forefront of global real estate investment conversations (Bitton, 2023). However, we should remember what Warren Buffet said: "Be fearful when others are greedy and to be greedy only when others are fearful" (Brownlee, 2023, p. 1).

SECTION 6: A CASE STUDY OF A SUCCESSFUL REIT AND A PITFALL

Case Study of a Success: Digital Reality

A prominent REIT specializing in data center ownership and management showcased impressive financial performance in Q2 2023. The company strategically capitalizes on the global shift towards cloud computing and the increasing importance of data and artificial intelligence.

- Key Indicators and Insights:
- Financial Strength:
- *Metrics:* Robust leasing, favorable pricing environment, and liquidity exceeding $4 billion.
- *Investor Focus:* Indicates a strong customer value proposition and sustained growth, highlighting the potential for future success.
- Strategic Initiatives:
- *Initiatives:* Unveiling Data Gravity Index 2.0, commitment to ESG initiatives, and reducing global carbon emissions.
- *Investor Focus:* Emphasizes Digital Realty's pivotal role in supporting digital transformation and sustainable growth, enhancing investor confidence.
- Operational Growth:
- *Metrics:* Growth across multiple operational aspects.
- *Investor Focus:* Demonstrates sustained momentum in a dynamic environment, reinforcing the company's strategic positioning.

Digital Realty's success in the data center REIT sector is attributed to its strategic initiatives, financial acumen, and commitment to sustainable growth. The company's performance reflects its strong positioning for future success in the evolving digital landscape (Motley Fool Transcribing, 2023).

Case Study of a Pitfall: CBL & Associates Properties

CBL & Associates Properties, a REIT focused on malls in the Southeastern U.S., faced significant challenges due to the rise of online shopping, leading to reduced foot traffic, tenant bankruptcies, and, ultimately, Chapter 11 bankruptcy in 2020.

- Key Issues and Lessons:
- Over-Reliance on a Single Sector:
- *Challenge:* Heavy concentration in malls and traditional retail.
- *Outcome:* Severe impact on rental income and financial distress, highlighting the risks of over-reliance on a single sector.
- External Disruptions:
- *Factor:* Seismic shift towards online shopping.
- *Lesson:* External industry shifts can have profound consequences, emphasizing the need for diversified portfolios.
- Bankruptcy Filing:
- *Outcome:* Filed for Chapter 11 bankruptcy in 2020.
- *Cautionary Tale:* Illustrates the potential downfall of REITs heavily invested in sectors facing disruptive changes.

CBL & Associates Properties serves as a cautionary tale, emphasizing the importance of diversification and adaptability in the face of industry shifts and external disruptions (Reuters Staff, 2020).

Summary

In this chapter, the focus is on REITs. The narrative uncovers the sector's complexities, going beyond the stereotype of property ownership by magnates. The evolution of Commercial REITs, their unique tax structure, and recent challenges due to global shifts are explored. Major players like Growthpoint Properties and Redefine Properties dominate, while smaller entities bring diversity.

- Section 2 highlights the Advantages of REITs, positioning them as a bridge between commercial real estate and publicly traded stocks. The emphasis is on historical performance, income distribution mandates, and unique perks, making them popular among investors.
- Section 3 debunks myths around REITs, addressing misconceptions about capital requirements, risk levels, and the necessity of prior experience. It encourages potential investors to explore diverse opportunities.
- Section 4 explores legal frameworks globally, focusing on Malta's adoption of a REIT framework. Associations related to REITs are explored, offering valuable resources and support.
- Section 5 discusses recent trends, emphasizing REITs' growing significance, economic impact, global adoption, and the importance of effective valuation.
- Section 6 presents a case study of a Successful REIT (Digital Realty) and a Pitfall (CBL & Associates Properties), highlighting key indicators and lessons.

In the next chapter, you are invited to lay a solid foundation for maximizing returns and mitigating risks in Real Estate Investment Trusts.

CHAPTER 3

BUILDING YOUR REIT FOUNDATION

EMBARKING on the REIT journey means traversing a bridge between two realms: the solid reliability of real estate and the dynamic flux of stock markets. REITs symbolize a blend of old and new. One side represents tangible real estate assets, like towering skyscrapers, buzzing shopping malls, and expansive industrial hubs that have always signified growth and stability. Conversely, the stock market epitomizes the modern world's pulsating rhythm, where every tick can lead to profit or loss.

REITs serve as a nexus between these diverse spheres. They allow both veteran investors and financial novices to transition from the solidity of real estate to the quick-paced world of stock trading. This union brings together the tangibility of ancient cities with the vibrant energy of modern financial hubs. Thus, investors get a unique proposition: the tangible allure of property coupled with stock market fluidity.

The blend REITs offer is crucial. Relying only on real estate could mean forgoing the agility and diversification of stock markets. While tangible assets promise security, stock markets offer lucrative quick gains but have their own volatility.

REITs' brilliance is their bridging capability. They provide a balance, enabling investors to enjoy both real estate's stability and the stock market's dynamism. This blend ensures that investors need not to compromise. They get real estate's reassuring physical presence and the stock market's dynamic potential. For seasoned investors, REITs mix familiar terrain with new possibilities. Meanwhile, newcomers find a safe yet promising initiation into the investment world in REITs.

SECTION 1: SETTING INVESTMENT GOAL

Defining Financial Independence

Pursuing financial freedom is a journey many embark on but achieved by a select few. There are numerous reasons for this disparity: a lack of information, inadequate planning, or lack of actionable strategies. However, the journey to financial independence becomes much more navigable when armed with the proper knowledge. In the vast realm of financial instruments, REITs have emerged as a potent tool for those looking to build a robust investment portfolio (Probasco, 2023).

- The Quintessence of Financial Freedom

Financial independence is not merely about accumulating vast wealth but ensuring that it allows one to live on their own terms. This could translate to enjoying vacations without looking at price tags, ensuring your children's education is not burdened by loans, or simply retiring without the fear of bills piling up.

- The Varied Shades of Independence

Financial freedom is not a monochromatic concept. A young professional might view it as the ability to rent their own apartment without parental aid. Meanwhile, a middle-aged individual might interpret it as the capacity to finance their child's overseas education without loans. The goals can be as diverse as ensuring a comfortable retirement, traveling the world, or philanthropic ambitions like supporting cherished causes.

- Navigating the REIT Landscape for Stability

Investment in real estate has long been viewed as a pathway to wealth creation. However, the direct acquisition and management of property can be resource-intensive. This is where REITs come into play, offering investors a chance to tap into the lucrative real estate sector without the hassles of property management. They serve as a bridge, merging the tangible allure of real estate with the dynamic world of stock market trading.

- Envisioning Your Financial Timeline

Setting your sights on what you want in the immediate versus the distant future can significantly influence your investment strategy. Short-term goals could include buying a car, while long-term ones involve building a retirement fund. Both timelines demand distinct strategies and risk appetites.

Risk Tolerance Assessment

- Peeling Back Layers of Personal Risk Appetite

Investment is not a game of blind darts; it is a calculated endeavor where one gauges potential outcomes and determines if they are comfortable with the possible risks. For some, the very thought of losing a penny might cause sleepless nights, while others might be comfortable with short-term losses for potential long-term gains. Recognizing where you stand on this spectrum is vital.

- The Multifaceted World of Risk Tolerance

Numerous factors interplay to sculpt one's risk profile:

- Age: A person in their 20s or 30s might have a longer runway before retirement, allowing them to entertain higher-risk investments with potentially greater returns. As one nears retirement, the emphasis often shifts towards preserving capital and ensuring a steady income stream.
- Financial Health: A person with minimal debts and a stable income might be better positioned to handle investment volatility than someone juggling multiple financial obligations.

- Future Financial Commitments: Upcoming life events, be it higher education, a wedding, or buying a home, can influence how much risk one is willing to shoulder.
- Striking the Right Balance with REITs

REITs, though a potent financial tool, are not devoid of risks. Market fluctuations, regulatory changes, or broader economic factors can impact their performance. Investors need to strike a balance by diversifying their REIT investments across various sectors or geographies, ensuring that potential downturns in one area do not severely impact their entire portfolio.

Laying Down a Tactical Blueprint

- Crafting Financial Milestones

Setting ambiguous goals like 'I want to be rich' often leads to inertia. Instead, quantifying objectives lends clarity. For instance, aiming to accumulate a specific sum by a certain age for retirement gives direction to one's investment journey.

- Asset Allocation

Just as knights need varied weapons in their armory, an investor's portfolio should be diverse. Beyond REITs, this could encompass stocks, bonds, savings accounts, cryptocurrencies, or entrepreneurial ventures. Each asset class has its risk-reward profile, and distributing investments across them can help mitigate risks.

- Skill as an Intangible Asset

While financial assets undoubtedly play a pivotal role, one should recognize the value of knowledge. In today's information age, upskilling oneself, understanding market dynamics, or acquiring knowledge about newer investment avenues can be a game-changer.

- Operational Strategies

Crafting a budget that details income streams and expenses provides a snapshot of one's financial health. Such clarity can spotlight areas where expenses can be trimmed, creating room for more savings and investments. Furthermore, leveraging tools like employer-provided retirement plans or tax-saving instruments can accelerate the journey to financial independence.

The Unwavering Spirit of Perseverance

- The Marathon, Not a Sprint

The pursuit of financial independence is relentless. It demands an artist's meticulousness, a monk's patience, and a warrior's resilience. Constant vigilance is imperative to avoid potential financial pitfalls.

- Adapting to the Ever-Evolving Financial Landscape

The world of finance is in a state of flux. Economic dynamics, geopolitical events, or technological innovations can disrupt established norms. Hence, periodically revisiting and revising one's financial strategy becomes crucial.

Navigating Personal and Investment Goals: The Interplay of SMART Goals and REIT Investments

Ambitions, whether in personal life or investment realms like real estate, have always been an innate human trait. What often differentiates successful endeavors from mere aspirations is a concrete roadmap. In the realm of personal development, the SMART goals serve as this roadmap. Meanwhile, crafting realistic ROI expectations becomes essential in the investment world, especially when dealing with REITs. Though distinct, these avenues emphasize clarity, realistic expectations, and actionable strategies. With integrative insights from some authentic sources (Mind Tools Content Team, n.d.; and Ghosh, 2021), we learn this.

The Essence of Goal Setting and Investing

- Delineating Objectives with SMART Goals

The SMART goals framework demonstrates that setting a clear, actionable, and achievable target is crucial. A goal should be: This precision ensures every effort is directed and purposeful, preventing aimless endeavors and offering a sense of direction.

- Specific: Clearly defined objectives with answers to 'W' questions.
- Measurable: Quantifiable metrics to track progress.
- Achievable: Grounded in reality and within capabilities.
- Relevant: Aligned with broader life or career objectives.
- Time-bound: With a clear timeline for execution.
- Navigating the Real Estate Sector with REITs

Not every investor can directly venture into tangible real estate due to capital constraints. This is where REITs come into play, offering an opportunity to invest in a diversified portfolio of commercial real estate assets without heavy capital outlay. But how does one navigate this avenue?

- Understanding Returns: Unlike direct real estate investments, which might promise soaring returns, REITs usually deliver realistic ROI, typically in the range of 7-8% annually after fund management fees.
- Entry and Diversification: REITs provide a low barrier to entry, making them accessible to small investors. They also promise safety, limited liability, and diversification, reducing risk.

- Asset Allocation: A significant portion, like 80%, might be invested in completed projects, whereas a smaller section, around 20%, is diversified into other avenues (Ghosh, 2021).

SECTION 2: RESEARCHING COMMERCIAL REITS

According to a study by Okoro and Ayaba (2023), the allure of real estate as an investment has remained undeniable over the years. While direct property investment requires significant capital, REITs have emerged as a beacon for those looking to invest in real estate without the massive upfront cost. Born in the United States in the 1960s, REITs have, over the decades, established themselves as one of the most stable and attractive forms of investment on the global stage. However, as with all investments, REITs have seen their share of highs and lows, with global events like the financial crisis and, more recently, the COVID-19 pandemic shedding light on their vulnerabilities and opportunities in the aftermath of such global events.

The Landscape of REIT Sectors

The universe of REITs is not homogenous. They span across various sectors, each with its intrinsic benefits and risks. Some REITs specialize in a singular sector like retail or industrial, while others diversify their holdings across multiple property types. The decision to specialize or diversify affects the risk and return profile of the REIT. Different sectors have unique characteristics; for instance, industrial REITs might be influenced by manufacturing outputs, while residential REITs could be more sensitive to population growth and urbanization trends.

- Driving Forces Behind Commercial Real Estate Growth
- There is no denying that REITs have seen significant success, especially in established markets like the US, UK, Japan, and Australia. Their popularity is underscored by events such as the rapid fund accumulation in the Shenzhen stock exchange market. However, the global adoption of REITs varies considerably. While mature economies have fully embraced REITs and reaped their benefits, emerging economies are still in the process of recognizing and tapping into the potential of this investment avenue.
- Diving Deep into Sector-specific Benefits and Risks
- Each real estate sector offers a unique set of advantages to investors. For instance, retail REITs might benefit from consumer spending surges during festive seasons, while residential REITs might see steady growth in populated urban centers. However, these benefits come paired with sector-specific risks. While specialized REITs can offer potentially higher returns due to their focus, they might also be more susceptible to market downturns affecting their specific sector. On the other hand, diversified REITs spread their risks across sectors, potentially offering more stable returns.
- Global Economic Shifts and Their Impact on REITs
- REITs do not exist in a vacuum. Broader economic trends and events influence them. The global financial crisis is a stark reminder of how external economic factors can severely affect REIT performance. Even the seemingly invulnerable REIT market felt the tremors of the crisis. More recently, the

COVID-19 pandemic has posed challenges to REITs. While some sectors, like commercial real estate, faced hardships due to remote working trends, others, like industrial real estate, saw growth spurred by e-commerce.

Evaluating REIT Performance and Value

When contemplating an investment in REIT, it is paramount to understand its financial health and growth potential deeply. REITs come with financial indicators distinct from traditional real estate companies. This makes it crucial to grasp how REITs operate before any potential transaction, especially for those familiar with GAAP standards. To analyze a REIT thoroughly, create or choose an approach combining a broad outlook and intricate details. A 'Top-Down Analysis' starts by exploring foundational elements like the quality of properties owned and diversification techniques (Aamer, n.d.).

In the domain of REITs, specific specialized financial metrics hold the key. Unlike traditional GAAP metrics, these focus on the unique nature of REIT operations:

- Net Asset Value (NAV) gauges a REIT's overall value by assessing the difference between its assets and liabilities.
- Funds from Operations (FFO) gives insights into a REIT's operational cash flow, adjusting for factors like property depreciation, which is not reflected in traditional net income.
- Adjusted Funds from Operations (AFFO) further refines the picture by accounting for regular expenditures required for property maintenance and rent adjustments.
- Net Operating Income (NOI) highlights the income generated strictly from property operations, providing a cleaner look at the profitability of a REIT's core operations.

For a 'Bottom-Up Analysis', understanding the value becomes paramount. Multiple valuation models can be employed:

- NAV Model assesses the market value of a REIT's portfolio using capitalization rates.
- The price-to-FFO model benchmarks a REIT's value against similar entities in the market.
- Dividend Discount Model (DDM) values a REIT based on its future dividend potential.

Utilizing multiple valuation methods provides a comprehensive understanding of a REIT's standing in the market. It aids in determining whether the offered securities are rightly priced and evaluates the prospective trajectory of the REIT's share price. Understanding the metrics' significance enables individuals to interpret authoritative research from reputable analysts on any REIT. For example, Morgan Stanley utilizes these financial metrics to present historical performance, present status, future trends, forecasts, valuation approaches, and potential risks.

Due Diligence Checklist

To comprehensively analyze a potential investment, especially when considering REITs, a meticulous checklist is vital. This list is not exhaustive but is a foundation for further exploration (Brainyard, n.d.).

- Evaluating Assets & Portfolio
- At the heart of every REIT lies its property portfolio. Ensure thorough examination of:

  ○ General corporate documentation, such as articles of incorporation, minute book, and business plan.
  ○ Comprehensive details of owned or leased properties, including the value, age, and quality of assets.

○ Real estate-related contracts, deeds, appraisals, and any relevant documentation.

○ Information about the physical environment, including environmental compliance and potential risks.

- Debt & Equity Structure Analysis
- An understanding of a REIT's financial standing requires:

○ Assessment of capitalization documents.

○ Scrutiny of debt financing documents like loan agreements, credit agreements, and promissory notes.

○ Inspection of equity financing documents, including stock purchase agreements.

○ Review of the company's general ledger, ensuring proper tracking of financial transactions.

- Legal & Regulatory Scrutiny
- Uncovering potential regulatory or legal issues before investment is essential. Look out for:

○ Regulatory documents, including governmental licenses, permits, or consents.

○ Legal documents, from pending litigation files to contracts.

○ Any previous or current government investigations.

○ Intellectual property documents, including patents, trademarks, and proprietary software details.

Section 3: The Art of Portfolio Diversification

Diversification in REITs

- Why Not to Focus Solely on One Sector

  o Concentration in a single sector can pose significant risks to one's investments. The ever-changing economic dynamics mean sectors react differently to market fluctuations. Ensuring a diversified REIT investment across retail, residential, commercial, and industrial sectors can balance the effects of any individual sector's performance, thereby safeguarding overall investments.

- Sector Diversification

  o The strategy of diversification involves spreading investments across multiple sectors. For instance, while the technology sector may dip, real estate or commodities might be on the rise. By diversifying across sectors like retail, residential, commercial, and industrial REITs, investors can navigate sector-specific risks and leverage opportunities that arise in each.

- Geographic Diversification

  ○ Geographical diversification goes hand-in-hand with sector diversification. Investing in REITs across diverse regions lets one tap into each area's unique real estate market dynamics. However, with global reach comes the challenge of managing currency risks, especially in international REITs. By understanding regional real estate trends and economic indicators, one can make more informed decisions and capitalize on geographical diversification benefits.

- Diversity in Property Types

  ○ Beyond conventional real estate categories, REITs offer investment opportunities in specialized niches like data centers and healthcare facilities. While generalized REITs provide broad exposure, specialized REITs can offer unique advantages, especially in booming sectors. Given the constantly changing economic landscape, periodically adjusting your property type mix can ensure you stay ahead of the curve and optimize returns (Ndirangu, 2023).

SUMMARY

The landscape of REITs bridges the concrete world of real estate with the dynamic realm of stock markets, offering investors both stability and the thrill of market dynamics. Recognizing the importance of diversification, the chapter emphasized the potential risks of concentrating investments in a single sector, advocating for diversification across sectors, geographies, and property types. It also highlighted the value of setting precise, measurable financial goals and illustrated the need for in-depth research before embarking on REIT investments.

Key insights included:

- The intrinsic value of REITs as a harmonious merger of real estate's tangible security and stock market fluidity.
- Defining financial independence as a multifaceted concept, varying with individual life stages and aspirations.
- The strategic benefit of employing top-down and bottom-up analysis methods to evaluate a REIT's financial and operational health.
- The emphasis on the necessity of due diligence and a meticulous examination of assets, legal implications, and debt structures.
- Diversification is the linchpin for a resilient investment strategy, encompassing sector, geographical, and property type considerations.

While understanding the intricacies of REITs and the significance of diversification is pivotal, translating this knowledge into actionable strategies is the next step. The forthcoming chapter will dive into the practical aspects of designing a robust REIT investment plan. From recognizing potential investment opportunities to crafting a portfolio aligned with individual financial goals, I will guide you in designing your roadmap to financial freedom.

PART TWO
STRATEGIES FOR REIT SUCCESS

CHAPTER 4

CRAFTING YOUR REIT INVESTMENT BLUEPRINT

INVESTING IS NOT SOLELY about seeking ways to amass wealth; it is also fundamentally about preserving your accumulated wealth. When done strategically, this preservation not only maintains your assets but also ensures their stability, even in fluctuating market conditions.

Balancing, expanding your portfolio, and safeguarding are crucial in the quest for financial freedom. This equilibrium can be finely tuned by incorporating insightful investment strategies, such as hedging. Hedging, at its core, functions as a financial safeguard (The Investopedia Team, 2022). Many might visualize 'hedging' as a garden fence that protects your plants. However, it is akin to an insurance policy in the finance domain. While it might not prevent negative occurrences in your investment journey, hedging acts as a buffer, mitigating the financial repercussions of such downturns. The hedging process involves the simultaneous use of complementary financial instruments or strategies. The objective is clear: minimize the risk of unfavorable price movements in your primary investment (Minogue, 2023).

SECTION 1: RISK MITIGATION STRATEGIES

Hedging Techniques

A deeper exploration into hedging techniques reveals the common use of derivatives, such as options and futures. Take, for instance, an investor who owns a particular stock. If there is apprehension about potential short-term losses, they might buy a put option as a protective measure. This mechanism ensures that even if the stock's price experiences a downturn, the losses on the stock are offset by the gains from the put option. Another practical illustration can be found in the business world. Companies often rely on raw materials whose prices fluctuate. They might opt for a futures contract to circumvent the unpredictability of these prices. This contract allows the purchase of the raw material at a predetermined price at a future date, ensuring cost stability. However, like all strategies, hedging has its limitations. It is essential to recognize that there is always a trade-off. The protection offered by hedging comes with its costs. While the primary allure of hedging is the reduction of potential losses, it is not tailored to maximize gains. In fact, in some scenarios, it might even limit potential profits. Moreover, unlike traditional insurance, which often guarantees full compensation after an adverse event, hedging does not promise a foolproof shield. It is a protective measure, yes, but not a flawless one.

Even if an individual investor opts to sidestep hedging, its understanding remains paramount. This is because many entities, from mammoth corporations to niche investment funds, employ hedging as a cornerstone strategy in the vast financial ecosystem. Whether it is an oil conglomerate hedging against volatile oil prices or an international mutual fund safeguarding against whimsical foreign exchange rates, the tentacles of hedging are widespread. Beyond mere protection, hedging also carves out a strategic niche. By offering a more transparent lens on future costs, hedging becomes an invaluable financial forecasting and budgeting tool. This clarity, in turn, seamlessly aligns with broader organizational goals, ensuring a harmonious synergy between micro strategies and macro objectives. A structured approach is vital for institutions eager to tap into the potential of hedging. This encompasses setting unequivocal policies, marshaling dedicated teams for initiation and oversight, and fostering a culture of transparent communication.

Defensive REITs: Stability in Market Turbulence

REITs have demonstrated varying reactions to economic shifts and market turbulence. As mentioned earlier, the recent economic downturn, brought about by global events such as the COVID-19 pandemic, has elucidated the significance of defensive REITs—those sectors within the REIT spectrum that are inherently stable even during market downturns. In March 2020, as the world grappled with the repercussions of the COVID-19 outbreak, global economies and stock markets faced massive disruptions. Notably, the S&P 500 encountered a drawdown of 32% from its peak. Meanwhile, the Dow Jones U.S. Select REIT Total Return Index, traditionally viewed as a defensive index, descended by 42%. Yet, it is essential to understand that the reactions within various REIT sectors were not uniform. Each sector's inherent stability or vulnerability was contingent on the type of property it was grounded in and its correlation with market conditions. For instance, sectors tightly knit with consumer spending, such as hotels and malls, faced significant blows. Their dependency on facets like travel, dining, shopping, and lodging made them particularly susceptible to the pandemic-induced economic slump. Specifically, hotel and retail REITs saw over 50% loss during that month.

Healthcare REITs, on the other hand, which majorly invest in medical offices and senior housing, declined by about 44.7%. It was observed that medical facilities, due to increased hospital visits, held their ground better than senior housing. The latter suffered primarily because its primary demographic—the seniors—were at higher risk and postponed moving into these communities. The growing work-from-home trend also impacted office REITs, causing a 34.5% sell-off as demand for office spaces dwindled. However, in this turbulent landscape, some REIT sectors showcased commendable resilience. Data centers and cell towers, essential infrastructures in the digitized age, experienced limited sell-offs. The reason was apparent: the rise in remote working amplified the need for robust internet connections, data storage, and consistent mobile usage. As a result, both sectors saw declines of only -8.8% and -12.9%, respectively, within the same period. Furthermore, the e-commerce surge favored industrial REITs, allowing them to outperform the market by 4.1%. Another beneficiary of the changing landscape was self-storage REITs, which gained traction due to the abrupt closure of educational institutions, resulting in a nationwide demand for storage solutions (S&P DOW JONES INDICES, 2020).

Monitoring and REITs Performance Adjustment

According to a study by Pfeffer (2008), Real estate markets are known for their cyclical nature. This poses a unique challenge for industry experts and scholars, especially in understanding how stock markets reflect real estate fundamentals. As the financial landscape has experienced upheavals, the emphasis on tracking and adjusting strategies based on REIT performance has grown. Tobias Pfeffer's comprehensive study from 1995 to 2006 delves into this challenge, examining the connection between real estate market cycles and REIT performance. Due to the intricate relationship between real estate and financial cycles and the need for vast data to conclude, Pfeffer's research is pioneering in its comprehensive analysis of REIT sectors and companies based on market performance.

Despite the limited historical data for REITs in regions like Germany and Europe, Pfeffer's analysis predominantly concentrates on the matured U.S. REIT market. It amalgamates data spanning 49 U.S. local markets, including major metropolitan areas, across sectors like Office, Industrial, Retail, Apartment, and Hotel. The dataset encompasses 131 REIT companies, capturing 75% of Equity REITs' market capitalization and over 30,000 individual properties, assessing factors like occupancy and rent alterations from 1995 to 2006. One of the standout revelations from Pfeffer's work is the varying time lapses between alterations in rent and occupancy versus changes in REIT earnings for different property type sectors. For instance, Office REITs showcased the strongest correlation between changes in market occupancy and their earnings after six quarters. Conversely, Hotel and Retail REITs indicated extremely short lags, sometimes none. Furthermore, the study demonstrates that while real estate cycles significantly influence REIT earnings, stock market pricing often diverges from these earnings, influenced by external factors like investor sentiment.

The research also probes into the capabilities of REIT managers to surpass the overall market in terms of enhanced occupancy levels and rent growth. Here, success is defined by the ability to time the market correctly and select optimal investment strategies. Findings indicate that, while REIT market performance typically aligns with the broader market cycle, most REIT managers were able to outshine the market. This superior 'market cycle performance' underscores the critical importance of REIT specialization concerning property types and market dynamics. Pfeffer's study is instrumental in its depth and breadth, marking a significant contribution to understanding property cycles and REIT performance. It not only paves the way for future research but also offers valuable insights for practitioners, especially in refining investment strategies and portfolio management for international investors.

Section 2: Building a Resilient Portfolio

Conservative vs. Aggressive Approaches

- Conservative Investing

Conservative investing is an approach that values the safeguarding of capital above the pursuit of high returns. Investors who lean towards this method typically prioritize stable and lower-risk assets, like blue chip stocks, fixed-income securities, and cash or its equivalents. Often, portfolios shaped by a conservative strategy will allocate more than half of their holdings to debt securities and cash equivalents, shying away from volatile assets. This method stands in contrast to an aggressive investment approach (Hayes, 2022).

- Key Features of Conservative Investing

The core principle is to maintain and preserve the purchasing power of capital with minimal risk exposure. Commonly, such strategies lean heavily on low-risk assets like Treasuries, high-quality bonds, money markets, and other cash equivalents. Adopting a conservative strategy can be influenced by several factors, including nearing retirement, prioritizing current income over growth, or anticipating a drop in asset prices.

- Understanding the Strategy in Depth

Conservative investors typically fall within the low to moderate risk tolerance bracket. As a result, their portfolios are characterized by a higher percentage of fixed-income, low-risk investments, complemented by a limited selection of high-quality stocks or funds. Treasury bills and certificates of deposit, regarded as the safest short-term instruments, are often part and parcel of a conservative investment strategy. While such a strategy can offer some level of protection against inflation, its returns might pale compared to more aggressive investment methods. Hence, as investors approach retirement, they often gravitate towards conservative investing, regardless of their risk appetite.

- Exploring Conservative Portfolio Strategies

Preservation of Capital: This aims to maintain the existing capital levels and safeguard the portfolio from potential losses. Instruments like Treasury bills and certificates of deposit are typical in this strategy. It is especially suitable for older investors wanting to optimize their current assets without incurring significant risks.

Current Income Strategy: Targeted at retirees with a low-risk appetite, this strategy seeks regular income streams without conventional salaries. It identifies assets that yield higher-than-average payouts, like dividends and interest. Although stable, current income strategies can be tailored to fit various risk levels. It is ideal for those interested in stalwart entities known for consistent payouts, such as blue chip stocks.

Even aggressive investors might temporarily pivot to a conservative approach in specific market conditions, especially if they foresee potential downturns due to market inflation or looming economic recessions. During such times, the move towards secure assets is termed a 'defensive strategy,' which emphasizes protection first and modest growth second. Once the market stabilizes, these investors might revert to a bolder, aggressive strategy. To counteract inflation's adverse effects on low-risk, low-return investments, conservative investors might consider assets like Treasury inflation-protected securities (TIPS) backed by the U.S. government.

- The Aggressive Approach

Compared to conservative methods, aggressive strategies, like a growth portfolio, generally promise higher returns. A growth portfolio, for instance, aims at maximizing long-term capital appreciation. Such portfolios might delve into riskier terrains like small-cap stocks, junk bonds, emerging international equities, and derivatives. A typical growth-focused portfolio might consist of 65-70% equities, 20-25% fixed-income securities, and the remaining assets in cash or money markets. Even though these strategies chase high returns, they are structured to offer some level of protection against severe financial setbacks. Investors well-versed in market dynamics and stock research might explore value investing portfolios rich in stocks or even consider passively managed exchange-traded fund (ETF) portfolios that blend stock and bond funds (Hayes, 2022).

Income-Driven and Growth-Oriented Strategies in Investments

An *investment strategy* is a personalized, dynamic plan to help individuals achieve their financial goals. Ranging from conservative to aggressive approaches, these strategies need regular reassessment due to the evolving nature of personal and market circumstances. Various factors influence these strategies, including age, financial goals, lifestyle preferences, and current financial standing.

- Factors Influencing Investment Choices:
- Age
- Financial goals (short and long-term)
- Lifestyle preferences
- Current financial standing
- Available funds for investment
- Personal circumstances (e.g., family structure)
- Risk Considerations:
- Risk is a pivotal factor in shaping investment strategies. Guidelines include investing amounts affordable to lose, the potential for higher returns in higher-risk scenarios, and the

trade-off between guaranteed capital preservation and minimal returns.

- Income-Driven vs. Growth-Oriented Strategies:
- Income-Driven: Emphasizes consistent income streams, suitable for those prioritizing regular income over capital appreciation (e.g., retirees investing in bonds).
- Growth-Oriented: Focuses on capital appreciation, involving higher-risk, higher-return investments (e.g., stocks or real estate), often preferred by younger individuals with a longer investment horizon.

- Aligning Strategy with Personal Objectives:
- Age and Goals: Younger individuals may opt for riskier investments with a longer recovery time, while those closer to retirement might favor a conservative approach for stable returns.
- Immediate vs. Long-Term Goals: Strategies differ for immediate goals (e.g., vacations) involving safer, short-term investments and long-term objectives (e.g., retirement) where riskier, growth-oriented assets might be considered.
- Essentially, the choice between income-driven and growth-oriented strategies depends on individual circumstances, goals, and timelines.

SECTION 3: CASE STUDY: A LOW-RISK SUCCESS STORY

The investment world is rife with high-risk, high-reward narratives. However, conservative strategies, too, have their champions. One such story is that of Alex Turner, an individual who achieved significant financial success by adopting a low-risk strategy focused on REITs. Alex Turner, a middle-aged accountant from New York, sought stability in his investments, steering clear of stock market volatility. Choosing REITs for a steady income stream, he implemented several strategies (Wachtell et al., 2020):

1. Diversification: Alex spread his REIT investments across various sectors, such as retail, healthcare, residential, and office spaces, avoiding concentration in one area.
2. Research and Due Diligence: Before investing, Alex meticulously researched each REIT, examining past performance, management quality, and dividend history.
3. Conservative Allocation: Initially allocating only 20% of his portfolio to REITs, Alex gradually increased his stake as he gained confidence, opting for a cautious approach.
4. Reinvesting Dividends: Instead of cashing in dividends, Alex reinvested them, capitalizing on the power of compound interest to enhance his long-term returns.
5. Staying Updated: Keeping abreast of market news, Alex adjusted his portfolio in response to sector-specific indicators, ensuring adaptability to evolving market conditions.

Outcomes:

- Alex's REIT portfolio consistently outperformed more aggressive stock portfolios over a decade, yielding a reliable 7% annual return.
- His REIT investments facilitated an early retirement, providing a steady income stream.
- During economic downturns, while traditional stock portfolios suffered, Alex's REIT investments remained relatively stable.

Lessons Learned:

- Patience Pays Off: Slow and steady strategies can yield significant returns without high-risk approaches.
- The Power of Compound Interest: Reinvesting dividends harnessed compound interest, significantly boosting the long-term value of Alex's portfolio.

- Staying Informed is Crucial: Continuous learning and staying updated are essential for making informed decisions in the dynamic investment landscape.

Alex Turner's journey serves as a beacon for risk-averse investors, highlighting that meaningful returns can be achieved with diligence and patience, even in unconventional investment paths.

SUMMARY

The chapter dives into crafting a successful REIT investment strategy by understanding the importance of wealth preservation and capital growth. The concept of hedging, akin to an insurance policy for investments, serves to minimize potential financial risks. A deeper dive into hedging reveals techniques such as options and futures. The chapter also underscores the significance of defensive REITs, which provide stability even amidst market turbulence. Various REIT sectors, including healthcare, office spaces, data centers, and more, responded differently to economic downturns like the COVID-19 pandemic. Monitoring and adjusting based on REIT performance, as studied by Tobias Pfeffer, is emphasized, revealing insights into market dynamics and how they reflect in REIT performance. The chapter also contrasts conservative and aggressive investment approaches, outlining the importance of aligning strategies with personal goals. The chapter concludes with a case study of Alex Turner, a conservative investor who succeeded with a low-risk REIT strategy. After understanding the nuances of REIT investment strategies and gaining insights from real-life success stories, the next step is to confidently arm oneself with the tools and knowledge to choose REITs. In the upcoming chapter, "Selecting REITs with Confidence," we will explore the specifics of REIT selection, equipping you with the expertise to make informed decisions and maximize your investment potential.

CHAPTER 5
SELECTING REITS WITH CONFIDENCE

TO EXPAND on what we have touched on earlier, real estate has long been acknowledged as an essential pillar in the world of investments, with its promise of steady income, long-term appreciation, and the potential to diversify a portfolio. This tangible asset has a rich history of safeguarding wealth against inflation and economic downturns. But in the modern era, investing directly in real estate properties requires significant capital, which becomes a barrier for many potential investors. This is where REITs come into the picture. They democratize the real estate market, making its advantages accessible to a broader audience.

REITs are companies or trusts that pool resources from various investors to purchase real estate assets. The beauty of a REIT lies in its simplicity. Instead of grappling with the complexities of direct property management, investors get an indirect stake in a plethora of professionally managed and curated real estate assets. This method not only simplifies entry into the real estate realm but also amplifies the potential benefits. For instance, as the properties under a REIT's wing appreciate in value, an investor's indirect stake in the REIT also witnesses growth, leading to capital gains. Various elements, including property improvements, changes in economic value, demand and supply shifts, and inflationary trends, can bolster this appreciation, creating a robust foundation for substantial returns. However, where does one begin when diving into the vast ocean of REITs? The starting point invariably revolves around a meticulous evaluation of fundamentals. Investors need to gauge the financial health of a REIT, looking for indicators like a strong balance sheet, positive revenue trends, and sustainable profitability metrics. Alongside the financial aspects, the expertise of the REIT's management team becomes pivotal. A competent leadership with a history of astute decision-making and strategic vision can make all the difference in navigating the complexities of the real estate market. Additionally, the quality and geographical diversity of the properties in a REIT's portfolio can provide insights into its potential resilience against market downturns and its capacity for growth.

Dividend safety is another cornerstone in REIT investment. Cash distributions from REITs, particularly those rooted in income-generating properties, offer a reliable income stream, often acting as an effective hedge against inflation. As property rents increase, reflecting inflationary trends, the resulting growth in cash flow can augment the dividends distributed to investors. This dynamic ensures a consistent income stream and contributes to capital preservation, further enhancing the appeal of REITs. However, the advantages of REITs are not limited to steady dividends and capital appreciation alone. The inherent nature of REITs offers investors a diversification avenue unparalleled by other asset classes. By pooling resources into a REIT, investors gain exposure to a vast array of property types and geographical locations. Such diversity acts as a protective shield, diluting the risk associated with any single property or market segment. When combined with the stability offered by real estate as an asset class, this positions REITs as an indispensable component for any balanced portfolio designed to weather market volatilities (Thomas, 2023).

Section 1: Evaluating Fundamentals

Financial Health REIT

A REIT is a specialized company involved in owning, operating, or financing income-generating real estate assets. They are known for distributing a significant portion of their profits, a minimum of 90%, as dividends to their shareholders (Harper, 2022).

- Understanding the REIT's Balance Sheet
- REITs primarily derive income from leasing spaces and collecting rents. Mortgage REITs, on the other hand, earn from interest on their investments like mortgages and mortgage-backed securities.
- A company must meet several conditions to qualify as a REIT. These include investing at least 75% of assets in real estate, cash, or U.S. Treasuries and earning a minimum of 75% of gross income from rents, interest on mortgages, or real estate sales. Furthermore, they must have a diverse shareholder base, with a minimum of 100 shareholders after their first year and

no more than 50% of their shares held by a limited number of individuals.

- Due to REIT status, these companies are exempt from corporate income tax, providing an incentive to distribute most of their profits as dividends.
- REIT Revenue Trends
- REITs can be categorized into Equity REITs and Mortgage REITs. Equity REITs own and manage properties, whereas Mortgage REITs deal with lending money secured by real estate or purchasing existing mortgages.
- Factors such as rising rental income, service income, and Funds from Operations (FFO) are considered positive indicators for revenue growth. The efficiency of a REIT's growth strategy, such as improving occupancy rates or increasing rents, can also play a significant role.
- Key Profitability Metrics
- Traditional metrics like earnings per share (EPS) and price-to-earnings (P/E) ratio may not be the best measures for REITs. Instead, analysts often use Funds from Operations (FFO) and Adjusted Funds from Operations (AFFO). These metrics adjust for non-cash charges like depreciation and mandatory dividend distributions.
- The net asset value (NAV) is another vital metric for REITs, aiming to replace the book value of a property with a more accurate market value estimate. Calculating NAV involves assessing the REIT's holdings, often requiring a somewhat subjective property appraisal.

Management Expertise in REITs

The effectiveness of REIT investments often hinges on the acumen and foresight of its leadership. To understand the sustainability and potential growth of a REIT, it is crucial to evaluate the management's approach, particularly its asset management strategies, which are geared towards optimizing investment profits. A comprehensive analysis was conducted on 41 REIT companies from leading markets like the United States, Japan, Singapore, Australia, and Malaysia. This analysis aimed to identify commonalities and differences in asset management strategies, comparing globally established REITs with those in Malaysia. The goal was to determine how these strategies align with best practices and literature on the subject.

Findings from this study can offer valuable insights for all REIT stakeholders, especially in understanding and implementing asset management practices that maximize investment returns. By looking at the successful strategies of REITs in developed nations, Malaysian REITs can glean guidance on adopting practical and effective asset management approaches. This research, one of the few of its kind, underscores the importance of strategic property investment within the REIT framework (Razali et al., 2021).

Property Quality in REITs

When evaluating a REIT, it is essential to consider its properties' quality and geographical distribution. However, the advantages of geographic diversification within a REIT's portfolio are debatable. A study from 2010-2016 on equity REITs showed a nuanced relationship between geographical diversification and a REIT's value. For more transparent REITs, meaning those with high institutional ownership or those investing in mainstream property types, geographic diversification is correlated with increased value. Conversely, a geographically concentrated portfolio is linked to higher value for less transparent REITs, those with lower institutional ownership, or those investing in niche property types. This value from diversification is primarily realized through operational efficiency at both the individual property and overall firm levels. Notably, the enhanced operational efficiency stemming from diversification, especially for transparent firms, is largely driven by superior revenue generation (Feng et al., 2019).

Section 2: Assessing Dividend Safety

Sustainable Dividend Metrics

When it comes to assessing the safety of dividends from an investment perspective, it is crucial to focus on specific metrics that indicate the potential for consistent payouts. Here are two key factors to consider (Hayes, 2023):

- Funds from Operations (FFO): One primary metric is examining the funds from operations (FFO) to ensure they cover dividend payouts. FFO represents the income generated by a REIT and is an essential measure for REIT investors. It provides insights into the financial health of the trust and its ability to meet dividend obligations. A healthy FFO that exceeds dividend payments is a positive sign of dividend sustainability.
- Payout Ratio: Another critical aspect is understanding the payout ratio and its implications for future dividend sustainability. The payout ratio is the total dividends paid to shareholders relative to the company's net income. In simpler terms, it is the percentage of earnings distributed as dividends. This ratio gives investors an idea of how much of a company's earnings are allocated to shareholders as dividends. A lower payout ratio indicates that a company is retaining more earnings for reinvestment or debt repayment, which can contribute to sustainable dividend payments.

Historical Dividend Trends

- Analyzing the Significance of Dividend History Assessment

In the realm of stock market investment, an indispensable element is the scrutiny of dividend history. The analysis of a company's historical dividend performance plays a pivotal role in enabling investors to gauge its past achievements and make well-informed decisions about its prospects. This section focuses on the importance of exploring dividend history analysis and its potential for yielding valuable insights (FasterCapital, 2023).

- Assessing Financial Stability

One of the paramount roles of dividend history analysis is to offer invaluable insights into a company's financial stability. A company consistently maintaining a steady dividend payout over several years signifies a robust financial foundation. Conversely, if a company's dividend payouts exhibit fluctuations, this may indicate financial challenges. Thus, scrutinizing a company's dividend history empowers investors to pinpoint businesses with financial steadiness and enduring growth potential.

- Discerning Dividend Growth

Dividend history analysis is instrumental in identifying companies with an unwavering tradition of dividend growth. A company that consistently elevates its dividend payouts year after year is more likely to continue this pattern. Furthermore, such a company attracts a more extensive investor base, potentially increasing its stock value.

- Evaluating Dividend Yield

Dividend yield, another pivotal factor in dividend history analysis, reflects the percentage of a company's stock price distributed as dividends. A high dividend yield implies that a significant proportion of the company's profits is returned to shareholders. However, a high dividend yield may also signify financial constraints that prevent the reinvestment of profits into the business. Consequently, evaluating a company's dividend yield in conjunction with its dividend payout history provides a comprehensive understanding of its financial health.

- Comparative Analysis

Dividend history analysis can also serve as a tool for comparing companies operating within the same industry. For instance, if two companies exhibit similar dividend payout histories, but one boasts a higher dividend yield, it could signal financial difficulties for the latter. Similarly, when two companies share comparable dividend yields, but one demonstrates a consistent history of dividend growth, it may suggest that the company with a history of dividend growth enjoys a more stable financial position.

- Comprehensive Assessment

In the realm of dividend history analysis, the optimal approach involves considering all the aforementioned factors while evaluating a company's overall financial standing. A company that maintains a consistent history of dividend growth exhibits financial stability and offers a reasonable dividend yield, which is often considered a promising investment. Nonetheless, it is vital to remember that dividend history analysis is just one facet of a company's comprehensive evaluation of growth potential. It should be complemented by examining other factors, such as financial statements and industry trends, to make well-informed investment decisions.

Identifying Dividend Risks

Recognizing Factors Contributing to Dividend Risks

In the investment world, it is imperative to recognize and analyze various forms of dividend risks that companies may face. These risks can stem from external and internal factors and are crucial for investors to understand. Here, we explore the intricacies of identifying dividend risks and how to assess them (Beers, 2022).

- Recognizing External Threats

One facet of dividend risk assessment involves identifying external threats affecting a company's dividend payments. These external risks may include economic downturns or sector-specific challenges. Economic downturns, for instance, can decrease a company's revenue and profitability, impacting its ability to maintain dividend payments. Similarly, sector-specific challenges, such as changing regulations or market disruptions, can pose risks to a company's dividend stability.

- Analyzing Internal Challenges

In addition to external risks, exploring internal challenges that may jeopardize dividend payments is essential. These internal risks often originate from factors within the company itself. One of the primary internal risks is high debt levels. Companies burdened with excessive debt may find it challenging to allocate funds for dividend distributions, as a significant portion of their earnings might be directed toward servicing debt. Poor management decisions can also hinder dividend sustainability. Ineffective strategies, misallocating resources, or inefficient operations can erode a company's financial health, affecting its ability to maintain dividends.

SECTION 3: REAL-WORLD CASE STUDY: SUCCESSFUL REIT SELECTION

This section presents a detailed case study of an individual who adeptly navigated the REIT market, showcasing the criteria, strategies, and reasoning behind their choices. We also analyze the outcomes, encompassing returns, dividends, and portfolio growth, and derive actionable insights for prospective investors (Infina, 2023).

Case Study: Mr. Pollonen's REIT Investment Journey

Meet Mr. Pollonen, an I.T. specialist who relocated to the United Arab Emirates in 2019. Possessing $500,000 in capital, he sought investment opportunities beyond purchasing a Dubai apartment, aspiring to achieve a Return on Equity (ROE) of approximately 7% per year, coupled with annual capital growth in the 7-8% range. Furthermore, he aimed to secure his investment and minimal exposure to draw-downs in the real estate sector.

To meet Mr. Pollonen's unique requirements, we devised a solution: a diversified portfolio of REIT stocks operating within the U.S. property sector. This portfolio was meticulously constructed, with companies assigned equal weightings based on market capitalization and price volatility. His investment holdings included Getty Realty Corp (5% allocation, ticker GTY), Vici Properties Inc. (24% allocation, ticker VICI), Iron Mountain Inc. (14% allocation, ticker IRM), Agree Realty Corp. (9% allocation, ticker ADC), Service Properties Trust (5% allocation, ticker SVC), CareTrust Reit Inc. (6% allocation, ticker CTRE), and LTC Properties Inc. (5% allocation, ticker LTC). Additionally, a 32% cash allocation was integrated into the portfolio, serving as a strategic reserve for capitalizing on opportunities resulting from better-than-expected earnings.

Subsequently, Mr. Pollonen found himself with a fully diversified portfolio, encompassing properties spanning from California to New York, catering to individual and corporate demands. These holdings delivered an average annual growth rate of over 10%, culminating in a remarkable 12% total growth on his investments, including a 3% growth on the cash reserve. Notably, the portfolio boasted a range of dividend yields, varying from 3.9% to 7.7%, and an average dividend yield of 4.35%, bolstering his cash flow.

By the end of 2022, Mr. Pollonen's astute investment strategy had elevated his portfolio's valuation to $715,000, reflecting fully rein-vested funds.

- Key Takeaways and Lessons
- Mr. Pollonen's investment journey underscores several vital lessons for prospective investors. Firstly, diversification is a cornerstone of prudent investing. By opting for a diverse

portfolio of REIT stocks within the U.S. property sector, he was able to achieve his financial objectives while mitigating risk.

- Secondly, seeking professional advice can be instrumental in guiding investment decisions. Mr. Pollonen's collaboration with investment advisors was pivotal to his success.
- This case study serves as a testament to the potential of REIT stocks as an attractive alternative for real estate investment, offering returns and dividends without the complexities and risks associated with traditional property ownership. Individuals like Mr. Pollonen can effectively pursue their financial goals and secure a more promising financial future by engaging with professionals and exploring various investment options.

SUMMARY

The chapter explores the realm of REITs and their significance in the world of investments. It highlights the historical role of real estate as a wealth-preserving asset, acknowledging its potential for steady income, long-term appreciation, and portfolio diversification. However, the modern era poses challenges, as direct real estate investment often demands substantial capital. This challenge is addressed through REITs, which democratize real estate investments, making them accessible to a broader audience.

The chapter underscores the simplicity of REITs, emphasizing that investors gain indirect ownership in a professionally managed and curated portfolio of real estate assets. The advantages of REITs include potential capital gains as the underlying properties appreciate in value, fueled by various factors like property improvements and inflationary trends. The chapter recommends starting with a meticulous evaluation of fundamentals to embark on a journey into the REIT world.

Investors are advised to assess the financial health of a REIT by examining indicators such as balance sheets, revenue trends, and profitability metrics. The expertise of the REIT's management team plays a pivotal role in their success, highlighting the importance of competent leadership. Furthermore, the quality and geographical diversity of properties within a REIT's portfolio are scrutinized to gauge resilience and growth potential.

This chapter also emphasized dividend safety as a cornerstone in REIT investments, focusing on metrics like Funds from Operations (FFO) and payout ratios. Historical dividend trends are valuable for evaluating a company's financial stability, growth potential, and dividend yield. Comparative analysis between companies in the same industry adds depth to the assessment. The chapter concludes by recognizing and analyzing external and internal factors contributing to dividend risks. A case study featuring Mr. Pollonen's successful REIT investment journey offers practical insights, highlighting the significance of diversification, professional advice, and the potential of REITs for steady dividends and capital appreciation. It encourages readers to explore the world of REITs as a viable alternative to traditional property ownership. In the next section, we will explore the wisdom and experiences of seasoned REIT investors. These individuals have navigated the REIT landscape, faced challenges, and reaped rewards. Their insights and stories offer a unique perspective on the world of real estate investments through REITs. The following chapter will explore the valuable lessons and strategies these veterans share.

UNLOCK THE POWER OF GENEROSITY

Make a Difference with Your Review

"Money can't buy happiness, but giving it away can."

FREDDIE MERCURY

People who give without expectation live longer, happier lives and make more money. So if we've got a shot at that during our time together, darn it, I'm gonna try.

To make that happen, I have a question for you...

Would you help someone you've never met, even if you never got credit for it?

Who is this person you ask? They are like you. Or, at least, like you used to be. Less experienced, wanting to make a difference, and needing help, but unsure where to look. Our mission is to make Commercial REIT Investing accessible to everyone.

Everything I do stems from that mission. And, the only way for me to accomplish that mission is by reaching...well...everyone.

This is where you come in. Most people do, in fact, judge a book by its cover (and its reviews). So here's my ask on behalf of a struggling potential investor you've never met. Please help that potential investor by leaving a review of this book.

Your gift costs no money and less than 60 seconds to make real, but it can change a fellow investor's life forever. Your review could help...

...one more individual understand the power of REITs.

...one more family secure their financial future.

...one more person step confidently into the world of real estate investing.

To get that 'feel good' feeling and help this person for real, all you have to do is...and it takes less than 60 seconds...

If you feel good about helping a faceless investor, you are my kind of person. Welcome to the club. You're one of us.

I'm that much more excited to help you Unlock the POWER of Commercial REIT Investing FASTER & EASIER than you can possibly imagine. You'll love the strategies I'm about to share in the coming chapters.

Thank you from the bottom of my heart.

Now, back to our regularly scheduled programming.

Your biggest fan,

Miles Bird

PS - Fun fact: If you provide something of value to another person, it makes you more valuable to them. If you'd like goodwill straight from another investor - and you believe this book will help them - send this book their way.

Scan the QR code to leave your review!

Review Link!

PART THREE
REAL STORIES AND STRATEGIES

CHAPTER 6

CONVERSATIONS WITH REIT VETERANS

THE WORLD of real estate investment can be both exciting and daunting. It is a domain where fortunes are made and lost, where every decision can shape your financial future. In this Chapter, we embark on a journey that promises to demystify the enigmatic realm of REITs through conversations with seasoned REIT investors. These individuals have not only weathered the storms of the real estate market but have also thrived, using REITs as their vehicles of choice. As we explore their experiences, we aim to uncover the wisdom and insights they have gained over the years. This Chapter serves as a platform to extract valuable knowledge from those who have walked the path, offering guidance and inspiration to both novice and experienced investors.

At its core, a REIT is a company or trust that specializes in pooling resources from various investors to purchase, own, operate, or finance real estate assets. The beauty of REITs lies in their simplicity. Instead of grappling with the complexities of direct property management, investors get an indirect stake in a diversified portfolio of real estate assets, all professionally managed and curated. This approach simplifies the entry into real estate investments while magnifying the potential benefits. When investors purchase shares or units of a REIT, they essentially gain a slice of a real estate pie that encompasses various property types, such as residential, commercial, industrial, or specialized properties. This diversity is a built-in advantage, offering exposure to different real estate market sectors. As the properties within a REIT's portfolio appreciate in value, the indirect stake held by investors grows in tandem, resulting in capital gains. Various elements, such as property improvements, changes in economic value, demand and supply shifts, and inflationary trends, can bolster this appreciation, creating a robust foundation for substantial returns.

Now that we have set the stage for our journey into the world of REITs let us explore the structure of this Chapter. We have engaged in conversations with seasoned REIT investors who have honed their skills through years of experience. These individuals have encountered the challenges, reaped the rewards, and accumulated wisdom that can benefit both novice and seasoned investors alike.

The conversations will revolve around key themes and insights. We will explore their investment journeys, from the initial steps to current positions. We will discuss their strategies and approaches to risk management. We will uncover how they have navigated the complexities of the real estate market and harnessed the potential of REITs. These interactions will provide valuable real-world perspectives that can inform your own investment decisions. In our conversations with these seasoned REIT investors, we will gain insights into their portfolio diversification strategies. We will discover their approach and how they allocate investments across different REIT types, including those focused on residential, commercial, industrial, healthcare, and other specialized properties. The experienced investor understands the value of a diversified portfolio, and we will explore how this diversity enhances returns and mitigates risks.

Risk mitigation is a critical aspect of any investment strategy, and seasoned REIT investors are well-versed in managing the risks associated with real estate investments. We will show how they handle external threats, such as economic downturns, market disruptions, and regulatory changes. We will also explore their methods for analyzing and addressing internal challenges, including managing debt levels, making strategic decisions, and optimizing property operations.

WISDOM AND STRATEGIES FROM ACCOMPLISHED REIT ENTHUSIASTS

This segment presents a series of interviews and discussions with seasoned REIT investors, delving into each investment journey, the challenges they encountered, and the strategies they employed to achieve success within the realm of REITs. The intent is to provide readers with firsthand insights into the REIT market, offering a practical comprehension of how to approach REIT investments and underscoring the significance of learning from those with practical experience in the field.

- Insights from a Seasoned REIT Investor: A Conversation with Paul Adornato

For instance, Paul Adornato, managing director at BMO Capital Markets, participated in a video interview during REITWeek 2017: NAREIT's Investor Forum at the New York Hilton Midtown. In the discussion, Adornato shared his views on the outlook for retail REITs, particularly in evolving consumer habits.

Adornato expressed optimism regarding the retail REITs' capacity to adapt to the changing landscape, emphasizing their strong relationships, a profound understanding of real estate, and robust balance sheets. He asserted that, over time, he anticipates retail REITs emerging as the frontrunners as the industry evolves.

Regarding the manufactured housing sector, Adornato anticipated that supply-demand dynamics would remain favorable. He attributed this outlook to stricter mortgage lending standards, which have led to limited credit access for single-family borrowers.

Notably, Adornato, set to step away from sell-side REIT research, observed that REITs have grown significantly in size and sophistication over the past three decades. However, he pointed out that there is still room for improvements to make the REIT industry more accommodating to shareholders. These insights and experiences from accomplished professionals offer valuable lessons for anyone navigating the world of REIT investments (Nareit, 2017).

- Insights from a Seasoned REIT Investor: A Conversation with Glenn Mueller

In an interview during REITWeek 2014: NAREIT's Investor Forum, hosted in New York, Glenn Mueller, a professor at the University of Denver and a real estate investment strategist with Dividend Capital Group, shared insights on various aspects of REIT investments (Borchersen-Keto, 2014).

- Journey into REITs
- Glenn Mueller, a seasoned expert in real estate investment strategies, discussed the historical volatility of REITs and their place in the investment landscape. He highlighted that while REITs are generally less volatile than the broader market, their volatility temporarily increased during the financial crisis, primarily due to the influence of exchange-traded funds (ETFs). However, as market conditions returned to normal, leveraged ETFs lost their influence, and REITs regained their low-volatility status.
- Diversification and Risk Management
- Mueller delved into the impact of index funds and ETFs on the REIT market. He noted that, historically, REIT investments were more restricted to individual investors and focused real estate funds. With the rise of indexed funds and ETFs, there has been a noticeable increase in correlation between REITs and the broader market. However, this has not diminished the essential benefits of REITs in diversified investment portfolios. Their higher dividend yields and stability in earnings make them a valuable component in real estate investments and a prudent choice for investors.
- Key Economic Indicators
- Discussing key economic indicators to watch, Mueller emphasized the significance of employment growth. Since the second quarter of 2010, positive employment trends have driven increased demand for real estate, resulting in improved occupancies and rents across various property types. Additionally, he highlighted the importance of monitoring gross domestic product (GDP) data, particularly for the hotel and industrial sectors.

Mueller's insights shed light on the enduring appeal of REITs, their role in diversification, and the crucial economic indicators that inform investment decisions.

- Insights from a Seasoned REIT Investor: A Conversation with Katie Barthmaier
- Journey into the World of Cannabis REITs

Katie Barthmaier, the CEO of GreenAcreage, an independently managed cannabis REIT, shared her remarkable journey into the realm of cannabis REITs. With an extensive background in net lease REITs, where she dealt with various specialized assets during her nearly 14-year tenure at W.P. Carey, Barthmaier entered the cannabis REIT space through an opportunity presented by David Carroll, a colleague of Acreage CEO Kevin Murphy. Her transition was motivated by the exciting prospects of the rapidly growing cannabis market (Pallardy, 2019).

- Building a Team of REIT Experts

The GreenAcreage team is comprised of seasoned leaders with extensive REIT investment experience. Gordon DuGan, formerly the CEO of W.P. Carey, now serves as the Executive Chairman of GreenAcreage. With significant investment experience, David Carroll holds the position of Vice Chairman. Jeff Lefleur, an 18-year REIT veteran, has taken on the role of chief investment officer. Chief Operating Officer Wilson Pringle and Chief Financial Officer Fred Starker bring their decades of experience to the team, adding depth to the management.

- The Power of a Strategic Relationship with Acreage Holdings

While GreenAcreage's roots are in its relationship with Acreage Holdings, it was always intended to be an independent REIT. Barthmaier stressed the importance of diversifying the REIT's portfolio to enhance its stability and provide a steady source of capital for Acreage and other industry operators. The strategic relationship has resulted in several closed property deals with Acreage, encompassing cultivation facilities in Pennsylvania and Massachusetts and a dispensary in

Connecticut. Another property, a build-to-suit facility in Florida, is in the works. Additionally, GreenAcreage has secured the right to make the first offer on Acreage's future real estate opportunities for the next few years.

- Deal Structure and Capitalization

GreenAcreage specializes in providing sale-leaseback and construction financing to the cannabis sector. The REIT positions itself as a long-term capital partner, focusing on 15- to 20-year lease agreements with cap rates typically ranging from 11 to 15 percent, complete with annual escalations.

- Expanding Horizons with Cresco Labs

GreenAcreage's foray beyond Acreage properties marked a significant milestone when it acquired a 220,000-square-foot cultivation facility from Cresco Labs in Illinois for $50 million. The REIT has already allocated $40 million and plans to invest an additional $10 million as the facility nears completion. The decision to invest in Cresco Labs was made based on a favorable view of their management, financial performance, and the potential of the Illinois market, which is set to embrace recreational cannabis use.

- Capital Raising and Diverse Investor Base

GreenAcreage has successfully raised $140 million, with $65 million already deployed in investments, split between Acreage assets and the Cresco cultivation facility. The REIT anticipates additional acquisitions in the near future. Its investor base includes a range of stakeholders, from hedge funds to family offices. Looking ahead, in Q1, GreenAcreage will likely seek new capital to fuel further growth.

- Future Investments and Expanding Horizons

GreenAcreage is keen on diversifying its portfolio by considering different asset types, geographies, and operators. While cultivation facilities remain central to its business, the REIT also eyes ancillary assets and production and testing facilities. Regarding geographical expansion, GreenAcreage closely monitors markets with high entry barriers and the potential for recreational legalization, including states such as Illinois, New York, New Jersey, Pennsylvania, Connecticut, Maryland, Arizona, Florida, and Michigan.

- Navigating the Evolving Landscape

In the rapidly changing cannabis industry, staying abreast of industry developments is challenging, but the evolving equity valuations have made alternative capital providers like GreenAcreage an appealing choice. While going public is a consideration for the future, no specific timeline has been set. Barthmaier emphasized that the team remains committed to diligently underwriting credits and entering into long-term leases to ensure their operator partners can meet their obligations.

As the cannabis industry continues to evolve, GreenAcreage stands poised to leverage its expertise, selective approach, and strategic vision to contribute to the sector's growth.

Veterinary REIT for Diversification

Terravet Real Estate Solutions has unveiled its inaugural private real estate investment trust (REIT)–Terravet REIT, Inc. The newly established trust, Terravet REIT, Inc., presents an avenue for veterinary property owners to diversify their real estate assets by participating in a pool anticipated to encompass numerous substantial general practice facilities and specialty/emergency veterinary hospital facilities across the United States, according to an official press release.

- Journey into REITs

The launch of Terravet's REIT marks an entry into the world of REITs, serving as a strategic move to address the needs of veterinary real estate owners. It offers a tax-efficient option for those property owners who recognize the value of their real estate but are hesitant to sell due to potential tax implications and other considerations.

- Diversification and Risk Management

By adopting Terravet's Umbrella Partnership Real Estate Investment Trust (UPREIT) structure, single-property owners can seamlessly contribute their facilities to this specialized veterinary-focused REIT. The UPREIT structure not only provides tax advantages but also opens the door to diversification opportunities and the potential for increased value and liquidity in the future. This approach allows veterinarians to benefit from the broader pool of veterinary real estate assets within the REIT.

- Key Economic Indicators

The REIT is under the governance of a board of directors and enjoys majority ownership by prominent figures in the veterinary sector. Partners include individuals such as Randy Bimes, DVM, who serves as the Chair of the Community Veterinary Partners Medical Advisory Board and is a member of the REIT's board of directors. This collaboration ensures that the Terravet REIT aligns with the needs and interests of successful veterinarians who seek to stay invested in veterinary real estate while also realizing the importance of diversifying their real estate portfolio.

Terravet Real Estate Solutions, with an existing portfolio encompassing over 1 million square feet of veterinary and healthcare real estate in 31 states, is renowned for its commitment to working closely with veterinary and healthcare operators to optimize property value through facility enhancements and real estate investments. The Terravet REIT focuses on purpose-built veterinary facilities, positioning investors to benefit from real estate tailored to the evolving requirements of veterinarians and pet owners in the modern era (dvm360, 2022).

SUMMARY

The Chapter engages in conversations with REIT veterans, where we embark on a captivating journey deep into the world of REITs, guided by the insights and experiences of seasoned REIT investors. These individuals have not only weathered the unpredictable tides of the real estate market but have excelled, utilizing REITs as their primary investment tool. The Chapter serves as an enlightening platform for extracting the invaluable wisdom and insights they have accumulated over the years, offering guidance and inspiration to both novice and experienced investors alike.

The Chapter begins by setting the stage for the significance of REITs in real estate investment. Real estate is a cornerstone of investment, historically celebrated for its reliability in generating steady income, long-term appreciation, and portfolio diversification. Yet, the hefty capital requirements for direct real estate investments often restrict access to only a privileged few. This is where REITs emerge as transformative equalizers, democratizing access to the benefits of real estate investment.

At its core, a REIT is a mechanism that pools resources from various investors to purchase, own, operate, or finance a diverse array of real estate assets. The simplicity of REITs allows investors to gain an indirect stake in a professionally managed and diversified portfolio of real estate assets. This indirect stake provides the potential for capital appreciation and a reliable income stream through dividends. Diversity is another key strength of REITs. By investing in a REIT, individuals gain exposure to different real estate market sectors, such as residential, commercial, industrial, and specialized properties. This built-in diversity protects against the risks associated with individual properties or market segments. When combined with the inherent stability of real estate, this makes REITs an indispensable component in balanced portfolios designed to withstand market volatility.

The Chapter's primary focus is on conversations with REIT veterans. It explores their investment journeys, strategies, and risk management approaches. These seasoned investors share their insights into portfolio diversification strategies, illuminating how they allocate investments across various REIT types. Risk mitigation, a critical aspect of any investment strategy, is also discussed, covering how they navigate external threats and internal challenges. These interviews serve as a treasure trove of practical knowledge, offering invaluable real-world perspectives for shaping investment decisions. Furthermore, the Chapter introduces insights from accomplished REIT professionals like Paul Adornato and Glenn Mueller, who share their views on retail and real estate investments. Additionally, Katie Barthmaier's journey into cannabis REITs exemplifies the growth potential in this evolving sector, demonstrating the significance of strategic vision in mastering the art of REIT investments.

Lastly, the Chapter explores the emergence of veterinary REITs as a unique opportunity for diversification. Terravet Real Estate Solutions introduces its inaugural REIT, providing veterinary property owners with a tax-efficient method to diversify their real estate holdings while maintaining their valuable real estate assets. Terravet's approach aligns with the interests of veterinarians looking to balance their real estate investments while safeguarding their wealth.

This Chapter presented a comprehensive exploration of examples in the world of REITs, bringing together the experiences of industry veterans, insightful discussions, and the evolving landscape of real estate investments. It equips readers with the knowledge and insights needed to navigate the challenges and opportunities within the dynamic world of REIT investments. In the next Chapter, as we journey through these discussions, I will equip you with the knowledge and insights to navigate the common pitfalls of REIT investments while learning how to master this dynamic investment landscape.

CHAPTER 7
OVERCOMING COMMON PITFALLS

THE WORLD of real estate investment is both enticing and complex. Within this realm, it is crucial to recognize that the path to mastering the art of REIT investments is laden with challenges and pitfalls that necessitate careful consideration. This comprehensive chapter explores the intricacies of REIT investments, highlighting the common risks and drawbacks associated with them, and offers guidance on how to navigate these challenges effectively.

LEARNING FROM PAST MISTAKES

The journey toward mastering REIT investments begins with learning from past mistakes, as highlighted by LinkedIn Real Estate (2023). Key pitfalls to avoid include market volatility, where REITs are influenced by factors like interest rates and economic conditions, leading to substantial price fluctuations. Liquidity issues pose a challenge, with varying levels of tradability and potential restrictions. Tax implications, such as treating dividends as ordinary income, may result in a higher tax liability than capital gains. The quality of management is crucial, as differences in competence, ethics, and alignment with shareholder interests can impact a REIT's success. Diversification limits emphasize that while REITs offer diversification benefits, investors should combine them with other assets for a balanced approach due to variations in property types, locations, and asset quality among REITs.

SECTION 1: LACK OF DUE DILIGENCE

Embarking on mastery in REITs requires careful navigation of pitfalls, particularly the risk associated with inadequate due diligence, as emphasized by MacBride (2011). The exploration dives into substantial risks arising from insufficient due diligence, including (Mabece, 2018):

- Inadequate Understanding of the REIT: Novice investors often need to pay more attention to the unique aspects of REITs, such as tax structures and distribution requirements, resulting in investments misaligned with financial goals.
- Ignoring the Property Portfolio: Neglecting analysis of the properties' types, locations, and quality within a REIT's portfolio leads to investments needing more diversification and exposure to specific economic risks.
- Neglecting the Management Team: Evaluate the competence, track record, and alignment of the management team to ensure investments are managed and aligned with financial objectives.
- Disregarding Financial Metrics: Key financial metrics like FFO, NAV, and debt levels provide insights into a REIT's health; overlooking these metrics hampers informed investment decisions.
- Failing to Assess Market Conditions: REITs are influenced by broader market conditions; ignoring these dynamics can lead to investments ill-suited for prevailing market environments.
- Overlooking Regulatory and Legal Factors: Regulatory and legal aspects impact a REIT's tax status and operational flexibility; neglecting them can lead to investments conflicting with tax planning or strategy.

- Ignoring Exit Strategies: Investors may overlook devising exit strategies for REIT investments, hindering the ability to capitalize on opportunities or protect gains.
- Emotional Decision-Making: Emotional turbulence, driven by fear or overconfidence, can lead to impulsive investment decisions that deviate from a rational strategy.

In all, avoiding inadequate due diligence is crucial for REIT mastery. Thorough research, ongoing analysis, and a disciplined, rational approach are imperative to mitigate risks and enhance prospects for success in REIT investments.

Case Study: The Hasty Investor

Let us consider a case study of 'The Hasty Investor' to underscore the critical importance of conducting due diligence when investing in REITs. This case study serves as a cautionary tale about the consequences of inadequate due diligence and the potential pitfalls of impulsive investment decisions in the world of REITs (CAGRFUNDS TEAM, 2018).

- The Rush into REITs

Just like in the world of marriage, investing in REITs can be likened to a courtship. When the markets are surging, it is akin to the butterflies in your stomach during the honeymoon phase. But soon, the realities of the market set in, and that initial excitement wanes. The recent market volatility has left many investors second-guessing their decisions. Some who hastily jumped into the world of REITs are now questioning the wisdom of their choices, while those who hesitated are contemplating if they missed the boat.

- Myths Leading to Hasty Decisions

In this scenario, we encounter various myths and misconceptions that lead to hasty investment decisions:

- Insurance Premiums Return: Some investors are enticed by policies promising to return their insurance premiums. However, they often need to pay more attention to the fact that only a tiny portion of their premiums goes toward insurance costs, and the rest is invested, yielding meager returns that may not even keep pace with inflation. The lesson here is never to mix insurance with investment.
- Unrealistic Expectations: In recent years, some investors have enjoyed substantial double-digit returns within a short period. While this can happen, it is important to understand that equities are prone to volatility, and high returns are not guaranteed consistently. Realistic expectations are crucial.
- Panic Selling: Just as you would not sell your house during a temporary price dip, panicking and selling equities at the first sign of negative returns is unwise. Equity investments are designed for the long term, and surviving market fluctuations is part of the journey.
- Guaranteed Returns: Guaranteed returns may seem comforting, but they are often close to or lower than the inflation rate. Such returns may preserve capital but will not help achieve long-term financial goals. Growing wealth requires calculated risks.
- Diversification: The belief that the highest returns can be achieved by concentrating all investments in a single instrument is a common misconception. The reality is that no one can predict the future with certainty. Diversification across different assets and instruments is a prudent strategy.
- Avoiding Daily Valuation: Technology provides real-time access to one's investment's daily valuation. However, constantly monitoring a portfolio can lead to restlessness. Just

as you do not regularly check your house's current value, equity investments require time to appreciate. Watching your portfolio daily may induce unnecessary anxiety.
- The Consequences of Hasty Decisions

In the case of 'The Hasty Investor,' the rush into REITs without proper due diligence resulted in financial losses, frustration, and missed opportunities. These investors now understand the importance of conducting thorough research, setting realistic expectations, and staying caught up to the allure of guaranteed returns.

SECTION 2: OVERLEVERAGING

Case Study: The Risky Gambit

In the realm of REITs, the concept of overleveraging becomes a precarious gamble, and it is essential to delve deeper into this idea through a case study referred to as 'The Risky Gambit." This case study unveils the perils associated with excessive borrowing when investing in REITs. In REITs, John had heard that REITs, on the whole, have strong balance sheets, making them a favorable investment option. He decided to put his money into REITs, hoping for solid returns (Askola, 2023).

- Leverage: The Double-Edged Sword

Before diving into John's story, it is crucial to understand the role of leverage in REIT investments. In this context, leverage is the use of debt to finance a REIT's operations and acquisitions. When used wisely, it can be a useful tool, allowing REITs to expand quickly and boost shareholder returns. However, like a double-edged sword, it can lead to severe consequences if mismanaged.

- Rising Interest Rates and the Warning Sign

John entered the REIT market during a time when the Federal Reserve was rapidly increasing interest rates to combat inflation. This rise in interest rates presented a warning sign for investors like John. High-interest rates can place a heavy burden on REITs, especially those that are overleveraged.

- The Changing Landscape

The good news is that, on average, REITs today are in a better position to weather high-interest rates compared to the 2008 financial crisis. Their leverage is lower, they have extended the average term to maturity for their debt, and they have increased the share of fixed-rate debt in their portfolios. This demonstrates that the industry learned from past crises.

- Identifying the Weak Links

However, not all REITs are equal. Some needed to prepare for the surge in interest rates, presenting higher risks to investors. As investors, it is essential to distinguish the strong from the weak in order to manage these risks.

- Five Overleveraged REITs

Now, let us explore the five REITs that John invested in, which, unfortunately, turned out to be overleveraged:

- Brandywine Realty Trust (BDN): This office-focused REIT was heavily concentrated in the Philadelphia market. The tenant mix primarily included traditional office space leased to industries that allowed remote work. This made downsizing by tenants upon lease expiration more likely.

Moreover, Brandywine was highly leveraged, with a significant debt maturity approaching.

- Office Properties Income Trust (OPI): Similar to Brandywine, OPI was another office REIT facing challenges. It leased a significant portion of its space to the government, and the budget deficit made it uncertain whether the government would consolidate its operations. OPI's leasing activity showed signs of distress and was highly leveraged, with substantial debt maturities looming.
- Vonovia SE (VNA): Despite having a positive outlook, Vonovia, a German apartment landlord, was significantly more leveraged than its U.S. peers. The low cost of capital and the unique German property market structure contributed to its high leverage. While it was not at immediate risk of bankruptcy, elevated interest rates posed a challenge.
- Cibus Nordic Real Estate (CIBUS): Cibus owned numerous grocery stores across Northern Europe, a seemingly recession-resistant business. However, its aggressive growth strategy in a low-interest rate environment resulted in high leverage and short debt maturities.
- Granite Point Mortgage Trust Inc. (GPMT): As a mortgage REIT, GPMT used a lot of leverage. The risk lay in its substantial office loan portfolio, which faced challenges with dropping office valuations. While not an immediate default risk, its high leverage magnified shareholder losses.
- The Key Takeaway

John's experience serves as a valuable lesson. Leverage in REITs is a double-edged sword. While many promising opportunities exist in the REIT market, the risk of overleveraged REITs must be considered. In the words of Warren Buffett: "It is far better to buy a wonderful company at a fair price than a fair company at a wonderful price." (Askola, 2023, p. 1). Therefore, it is prudent for investors to avoid distressed, overleveraged REITs and be highly selective in their choices.

Section 3: Neglecting Market Trends

Case Study: The Inattentive Investor—A REIT Perspective

In the case of the inattentive investor, the key to successful real estate investment in 2023 lies in a comprehensive understanding of the ever-evolving landscape of REITs. It is crucial to consider the challenges and opportunities the REIT sector will encounter in the coming year. The inattentive investor should take note of several essential factors that have been highlighted in this extensive analysis (Borchersen-Keto, 2022).

- Neglecting Market Trends: Macro Fundamentals and Market Volatility

Our inattentive investor should first acknowledge the significance of market trends in the real estate landscape. REITs' operating performance, driven by post-pandemic reopening tailwinds, was robust in 2022. However, the pace of growth is anticipated to decelerate in 2023. While macroeconomic conditions may remain challenging, including the looming specter of a potential recession, it is crucial to note that the fundamental underpinnings of the REIT industry remain relatively stable.

Leading portfolio managers in the field have shared their insights into the macro fundamentals shaping REITs in 2023:

- *Arthur Hurley* emphasizes the ongoing volatility caused by factors like rising interest rates, higher inflation, and recession fears. Inflation remains a concern, and investor focus centers on the Federal Reserve's ability to manage a 'soft landing.' Should the Fed succeed, REITs stand to enjoy attractive earnings growth. Given constrained new supply growth due to rising material and labor costs; real estate markets would benefit from steady demand.
- *Brian Jones* notes that, despite concerns about inflation, the broader economic trends in the United States are encouraging. Stable employment, solid income growth, and strong consumer and corporate financial positions should support real estate operating fundamentals in 2023. However, there is also the challenge of the Fed managing inflation trends.
- *Lisa Kaufman* anticipates a U.S. recession in the coming year but expects the Fed to succeed in taming inflation. The rise in rates has already impacted the REIT market. However, there is optimism for REIT returns in 2023 due to adjustments in real rates and the recent market re-pricing.

- *Rick Romano* underscores the continued macroeconomic challenges and the persistent volatility for REITs in 2023. However, he also highlights the importance of seeking answers to critical macro questions as a means to reduce risk premiums.
- *Jason Yablon* presents a nuanced perspective, anticipating a shallow, moderate-length recession and suggesting that inflation might have already peaked. He stresses the importance of sectors with pricing power and acknowledges that growth potential exists in various segments.

In summary, our inattentive investor must recognize the significance of macroeconomic factors, including inflation, recession, and interest rates, as they shape the REIT landscape in 2023. It is imperative to follow the insights of seasoned professionals and their assessments of economic trends and real estate sector potential.

- Public vs. Private Real Estate Investment: Navigating Market Disparities

Understanding the differences between public and private real estate investment is another vital consideration for our inattentive investors. The real estate transaction environment has shifted as buyers and sellers respond to the implications of higher interest rates and a potentially slowing economy. Both public and private real estate investors divert capital toward non-traditional sectors, such as data centers, cell towers, self-storage, and single-family rentals.

  ○ *Brian Jones* highlights the diversification of capital into non-traditional real estate sectors. REITs, characterized by less debt and more fixed-rate debt, may be better positioned to continue deploying capital.
  ○ *Rick Romano* underscores a substantial disconnect between public and private real estate markets, with private markets lagging in price adjustments. The private sector's need for

more pricing transparency has contributed to a slow transaction environment.

○ *Arthur Hurley* discusses the challenges of valuation visibility in the private real estate market, citing a disparity between buyer and seller expectations. In contrast, public markets have adapted more swiftly.

○ *Jason Yablon* focuses on how values are being recalibrated across both listed and private real estate as investors react to changes in the cost of capital.

In the context of our inattentive investor, it is crucial to recognize the nuances of public and private real estate markets. While the public market reacts more swiftly, the private market offers distinct opportunities and challenges.

- Property Sectors: Optimism and Caution for 2023

The next critical consideration for the inattentive investor involves assessing property sectors that show promise and those that raise concerns. Promising sectors include:

○ *Rick Romano* highlights property sectors with defensive characteristics, revenue growth surpassing inflation, and limited exposure to inflation on the expense side. Senior housing, in particular, benefits from reopening tailwinds and demographic shifts.

○ *Lisa Kaufman* expresses optimism about the residential sector, especially single-family homes. The upward pressure on rents, coupled with supply-demand dynamics, supports growth expectations.

○ *Brian Jones* and *Jason Yablon* both identify the potential of sectors like self-storage, single-family rentals, data centers, and healthcare, underlining the importance of pricing power and evolving market dynamics.

At the same time, some sectors demand caution:

> ○ *Jason Yablon* and *Brian Jones* caution against the office sector's
> uncertainties, particularly with the evolving landscape of
> remote work and shifting business travel trends. Retail also
> faces challenges, especially in the context of consumer behavior
> and inflation.
> ○ *Lisa Kaufman* expresses bearishness about the office sector
> due to the hybrid work environment's impact on demand. Also,
> the financial burden on landlords for sustainability require-
> ments and evolving corporate preferences presents challenges.

In 2023, the prudent investor must weigh the potential of different
property sectors, recognizing the sectors that offer growth opportunities and those that pose risks.

- REIT Mergers, Acquisitions, and Dispositions: The Changing
  Landscape

Understanding the dynamics of REIT mergers, acquisitions, and
dispositions is pivotal for the inattentive investor. Factors such as
access to capital and evolving deal financing have affected M&A deal
volume. Private equity firms are expected to explore go-private transactions, capitalizing on attractive pricing in the public markets and
abundant cash reserves.

> ○ *Arthur Hurley* underscores the challenges in deal financing
> and the attractiveness of the public markets relative to private
> ones. This could motivate private equity investors to announce
> more go-private transactions.
> ○ *Jason Yablon* notes the potential for private equity to target
> assets of listed REITs if listed valuations appear more
> compelling than private ones. Furthermore, private real estate
> portfolios seeking diversification may consider listed real
> estate markets.

○ *Rick Romano* anticipates a robust landscape for REIT M&A if public and private real estate pricing remains disconnected. There is an opportunity for consolidation, privatizations, and cross-border acquisitions, especially with the strong position of U.S. dollar-denominated real estate companies.
○ *Lisa Kaufman* emphasizes the potential for increased transaction activity as private real estate valuations adjust downward, and the capital on the sidelines is deployed.
○ *Brian Jones* highlights that 2022 has been an active M&A environment, driven by the volatility of REIT share prices and transaction opportunities as share prices align with intrinsic value.

In the case of our inattentive investor, comprehending the evolving landscape of REIT M&A and capital flows is essential for making informed decisions in the ever-changing real estate sector.

- The Evolving Landscape of ESG Issues

Environmental, Social, and Governance (ESG) considerations increasingly shape real estate investments. The focus on ESG issues is expected to shift in the coming years, demanding attention from investors and real estate professionals.

○ *Rick Romano* emphasizes the growing importance of ESG in real estate investment and the need to align investment guidelines with clients' ESG priorities.
○ *Arthur Hurley* highlights the increasing demand for environmentally responsible structures and the need for REIT management teams to adopt quantitative measures and actionable goals for environmental impact and social initiatives.
○ *Brian Jones* underlines the significance of addressing climate change and CO_2 emissions reduction targets in the ESG realm, particularly in the office sector.
○ *Jason Yablon* notes the focus on carbon transition, physical

climate impacts, and human capital management, all of which will be key facets of climate change risks and opportunities.

○ *Lisa Kaufman* acknowledges the improvement in ESG disclosure in the real estate asset class, making it easier for managers to evaluate and engage with management teams on ESG matters.

For the inattentive investor, awareness of the growing importance of ESG issues in real estate investment is essential. These considerations extend to environmental impact, social initiatives, and governance measures.

In conclusion, while grappling with a complex and dynamic real estate investment environment, the inattentive investor would be wise to consider the various dimensions of market trends, investment strategies, property sectors, M&A activity, and ESG considerations. To navigate the ever-evolving world of REITs effectively, it is imperative for the inattentive investor to heed the insights, strategies, and perspectives shared by experienced professionals and to remain vigilant and proactive in the face of the challenges and opportunities that 2023 will bring. This comprehensive understanding is vital to making informed and successful real estate investment decisions in the year ahead.

SUMMARY

This chapter comprehensively explores REITs, outlining the challenges and pitfalls associated with mastering the art of REIT investments. The content is organized into key sections.

- Learning from Past Mistakes:
- The journey toward mastery begins with acknowledging past mistakes in REIT investing. Pitfalls include market volatility, liquidity issues, tax implications, management quality, and diversification limits. Investors are advised to understand

external influences, assess liquidity, scrutinize tax implications, evaluate management, and avoid over-relying on REITs for diversification.

- Lack of Due Diligence:
- Emphasizing the importance of due diligence, the section details risks arising from inadequate research. This includes insufficient understanding of REITs, neglecting property portfolio analysis, overlooking management quality and financial metrics, ignoring market conditions, disregarding regulatory factors, overlooking exit strategies, and succumbing to emotional decision-making.
- *Case Study: The Hasty Investor*

  o Illustrates the consequences of inadequate due diligence, debunks myths, and highlights the importance of realistic expectations, patience, and diversification.

- Overleveraging:
- Explores the risks of overleveraging in REITs through the case study 'The Risky Gambit.' Leverage is portrayed as a double-edged sword, and the case study identifies five overleveraged REITs. Investors are urged to be selective and cautious in their choices.
- *Case Study: The Risky Gambit*

  o John's story cautions investors about the risks of overleveraging, emphasizing the importance of distinguishing strong from weak links.

- Neglecting Market Trends:
- This section underscores the importance of understanding market trends through the case study 'The Inattentive Investor - A REIT Perspective.' It covers macro fundamentals, public vs. private real estate investment, property sectors,

REIT M&A dynamics, and the evolving landscape of ESG issues.

- *Case Study: The Inattentive Investor—A REIT Perspective*

  o It helps to guide the inattentive investor to recognize market trends, including macroeconomic factors, public-private market disparities, promising and cautionary property sectors, REIT M&A dynamics, and the growing importance of ESG considerations.

The chapter concludes by advocating for a comprehensive understanding of the REIT investment landscape, encouraging investors to learn from past mistakes, conduct thorough due diligence, avoid over-leveraging, and stay informed about market trends.

The case studies offer practical insights for navigating the complexities of REIT investments, catering to novice and experienced investors. In the next chapter, we will explore tips and strategies for investing in Government REITs, , revealing how they can serve as a stable and rewarding component of a diversified real estate portfolio.

CHAPTER 8

BONUS CHAPTER: TIPS AND STRATEGIES TO GOVERNMENT REITS INVESTING

IN THE DYNAMIC realm of investment portfolios, the spotlight increasingly turns towards a robust and often underappreciated asset class—Government REITs. As we navigate through this comprehensive exploration, we unravel the intricate layers that define Government REITs and their pivotal role in shaping a diversified and resilient investment landscape.

• Are REITs Underrepresented in Your Clients' Portfolios?

In a market where commercial real estate is a fundamental asset class, the absence of REITs in client portfolios prompts a critical inquiry. As we dive into the financial landscape, recognizing that commercial real estate constitutes 16% of U.S. investments, we begin to unveil the strategic significance of incorporating REITs into the investment playbook. This is particularly crucial for the 83% of financial professionals who acknowledge REITs as a low-cost, effective, and liquid avenue for building diversified portfolios that span the entirety of the U.S. investment market (Are REITs underrepresented in your clients' portfolios?, n.d.).

• How to Diversify Your Portfolio Using Government REITs

In a market where assets increasingly correlate, the challenge for advisors lies in identifying instruments that diversify their clients' portfolios. Government REITs emerge as a compelling solution, backed by research indicating their low correlation with the broad stock market. Our exploration includes tangible illustrations of how these REITs enhance a portfolio's risk-and-return profile, providing meaningful diversification opportunities in both traditional and modern property sectors.

• Appropriate Allocation to Government REITs

Determining the optimal allocation to Government REITs is a critical aspect of portfolio management. We decipher the ever-evolving landscape of REIT utilization through insights from studies, expert recommendations, and the dynamic Morningstar Glide Path Model. From optimal allocations for investors with varying horizons to considerations of age and risk tolerance, we guide through the nuanced decisions surrounding Government REIT allocations.

- **Government REIT Utilization Among Financial Advisors**

While risks and opportunities continue to unfold, there remains a consensus among financial advisors on the enduring fundamentals that support the inclusion of Government REITs within diversified portfolios. We dive into this consensus, exploring the unwavering belief in the long-term value and stability that these REITs bring to investment strategies.

- **Research from Morningstar on Government REIT Performance**

Uncovering insights from Morningstar Fact Sheets spanning over five decades, we scrutinize the performance metrics that distinguish Government REITs. From their substantial contribution to wealth compared to bonds and other stocks to their role in extending the lifespan of assets for retirees, we explore the compelling data that underscores the resilience and longevity of Government REITs.

- **Spotlight on Postal Realty Trust and Easterly Government Properties**

Our journey culminates in real-world success stories, featuring Postal Realty Trust (NYSE: PSTL) from Nareit Staff (2019) and Easterly Government Properties (NYSE: DEA) (*Million easterly government properties...*,n.d.). These case studies provide tangible examples of the transformative power of Government REITs, from consolidating critical logistics assets to offering tax-efficient disposition options. These success narratives underscore the potent value these REITs bring to investors and the broader financial landscape.

As we embark on this exploration of Government REITs, the narrative unfolds as a strategic odyssey, guiding investors, financial professionals, and enthusiasts alike through the multifaceted terrain of real estate investments.

KEY FEATURES AND BENEFITS STABILITY AND INCOME

- **Shielded from Market Concerns**:

Amidst the ever-evolving dynamics of office and industrial property markets, DEA and PSTL distinguish themselves by navigating challenges with resilience. Their secret weapon? A tenant of unmatched reliability—the U.S. Government. The strategic choice to cater exclusively to government agencies has shielded them from the lingering uncertainties affecting their counterparts in the commercial real estate sector (Sismanis, 2022).

- **The Unmatched Tenant**:

The strength of DEA and PSTL lies in their unwavering focus on mission-critical U.S. Federal Agencies and the United States Postal Service (USPS), respectively. With 99% and 99.7% occupancy rates, these REITs enjoy robust lease income backed by the full faith and credit of the U.S. government. Uncle Sam's unparalleled creditworthiness is a formidable advantage, eliminating counterparty risks and ensuring a steady stream of rental payments.

- **Why Uncle Sam Matters**:

Having the U.S. government as an exclusive tenant has monumental advantages, creating an impenetrable moat around DEA and PSTL. The credibility of Uncle Sam as a tenant, universally recognized as the most trustworthy creditor globally, provides an unmatched level of security. These REITs face no counterparty risk or rent collection issues, making them immune to challenges experienced by "ordinary" REITs.

- **The Assurance of Stability**:

With a one-hundred percent occupancy ratio since its public listing, DEA boasts a weighted average lease term of 19.6 years. Its properties, purpose-built for agencies like the FBI, EPA, USCIS, VA, DHA, and USPS, ensure an enduring margin of safety. PSTL, with a 99.7% occupancy rate, may have a shorter lease term, but its cash flows remain secure, offering the flexibility to renegotiate leases at higher rates sooner.

- **Analyst Perspective and Smart Scores**:

Wall Street analysts provide a vote of confidence, granting DEA and PSTL Hold and Moderate Buy consensus ratings, respectively. Measuring the potential market performance, Smart Scores reveal promising outlooks for both REITs. Despite their unique qualities and high dividend yields of around 6.4%, DEA, and 6.3% PSTL, their valuations remain surprisingly reasonable, trading at 11.5x and 16.2x projected FFOs for the year.

NYSE: PSTL-Stability, Growth, and Tax Efficiency

Postal Realty Trust (PSTL) emerges as a resilient investment option, providing stability and reliable income streams in a fluctuating market. With a diverse portfolio of over thirteen hundred post office properties across the U.S., PSTL showcases the characteristics of an industrial/logistics REIT rather than a traditional office-focused entity.

Despite economic uncertainties, PSTL has maintained a strong record of dividend growth, pausing temporarily in May 2019 to strategically retain cash for future growth and balance sheet fortification. The commitment to a covered dividend and annual reviews for potential growth reflects a dynamic approach to navigating market conditions.

Essential to PSTL's income resilience is its strategic lease negotiations with the United States Postal Service (USPS), securing favorable terms and fixed annual rent escalations. These escalators are poised to contribute to future dividend hikes, aligning with PSTL's dedication to delivering growing returns to investors.

PSTL's tax-efficient dividend structure further enhances its appeal. Approximately 35% of the dividend is characterized as a Return of Capital (ROC) since its IPO. This not only lowers the current tax liability, providing investors with higher cash flow but also facilitates faster investment compounding for those reinvesting dividends (*Postal Realty Trust: Logistics Delivering...*, 2023).

Moreover, PSTL's tax-efficient gifting strategies offer a philanthropic avenue for investors. Reducing cost basis through ROC creates potential capital gains on share sales, presenting an attractive option for long-term holders seeking to make impactful charitable contributions.

NYSE: DEA : A Tax-Advantage

In its recent announcement on January 18, 2023, NYSE: DEA, leased to the U.S. Government, revealed the tax characteristics of its 2022 distributions. This tax reporting, accessible through Form 1099-DIV, provides investors with valuable insights into the specific tax treatment of the distributions.

Here is a breakdown of the key tax characteristics associated with Easterly's common shares distributions in 2022 (*Easterly government properties announces tax characteristics...*, 2023).

Record Date vs. Payment Date:

Record Dates:

- 3/10/2022
- 5/13/2022
- 8/11/2022
- 11/11/2022

Payment Dates:

- 3/22/2022
- 5/25/2022
- 8/23/2022
- 11/23/2022

Dividend Per Share:

- $0.2650 for each distribution

Tax Characteristics:

Ordinary Taxable Dividend:

- Total: $1.0600
- Percentage: 100.00%

Return of Capital:

- Total: $0.5032
- Percentage: 47.48%

Capital Gain:

- Total: $0.5568
- Percentage: 52.52%

Unrecaptured Sec. 1250 Capital Gain and Section 199A Dividend:

- Both totaling $0.0000

This comprehensive breakdown allows shareholders to gain a clear understanding of the tax implications associated with the distributions. It is important to note that the amounts provided are part of the Ordinary Taxable Dividend, emphasizing the transparency and accountability in tax reporting.

Investors are encouraged to consult their tax advisors for specific guidance tailored to their circumstances. As Easterly Government Properties prioritizes transparency and clarity in its communication, shareholders can confidently navigate the tax landscape associated with their investments in Government REITs.

Section 2: Assessing Investment Potential

- **Analyzing Financial Health**

Diving into their unique market positions is essential to gauge the financial stability and performance of Government REITs. Two relatively obscure yet promising entities, NYSE: DEA and NYSE: PSTL, stand out due to their adept navigation of challenges in the office and industrial property sectors. Both have strategically positioned themselves by catering exclusively to the most reliable tenant— the United States Government. Amid the uncertainties in the broader real estate landscape, DEA and PSTL have exhibited resilience, reflected in their high dividend yields and reasonable valuations. The assessment of their financial health should include examining their ability to weather market dynamics and challenges specific to the government real estate sector.

- **Portfolio Composition**

Understanding the types of assets held within Government REIT portfolios is crucial for assessing their long-term viability. DEA and PSTL have distinguished themselves by focusing on the niche of providing office space exclusively to U.S. government agencies. This unique portfolio composition shields them from the broader disruptions experienced by commercial real estate properties in the aftermath of the COVID-19 pandemic. DEA, for instance, boasts a portfolio comprising 92 operating properties leased primarily to U.S. government tenant agencies, with a remarkable 99% occupancy rate. PSTL, on the other hand, serves the USPS exclusively, emphasizing the stability that comes with having the U.S. government as the sole tenant.

- **What Sets DEA and PSTL Apart?**
- Unparalleled Credit of Uncle Sam

The distinctive advantage of having the U.S. government as an exclusive tenant forms a stronghold moat for DEA and PSTL. The creditworthiness of Uncle Sam is universally acknowledged, making it the most trustworthy creditor globally. This unique quality eliminates counterparty risk and rent collection issues, providing a substantial advantage over ordinary REITs. As mentioned earlier, with tenants including mission-critical agencies like the FBI, EPA, USCIS, VA, DHA, and USPS, the U.S. government's ability to print money to meet its obligations ensures a consistent and secure income stream for DEA and PSTL.

- **Long-Term Lease Agreements**

The extended lease terms contribute to the stability of cash flows for both DEA and PSTL. DEA, with a weighted average lease term of 19.6 years, and PSTL, with an occupancy rate of 99.7% and a weighted average lease term of approximately four years, offer investors an unparalleled margin of safety. The purpose-built nature of their properties for each agency's needs adds an additional layer of security, as relocation is not feasible for these essential government operations.

Analyst Ratings

- DEA and PSTL Stock Analysis

Analysts' sentiments on DEA and PSTL stocks provide further insights. DEA has a Hold consensus rating, with an average stock forecast suggesting a substantial upside potential of around 34.5%. PSTL, on the other hand, holds a Moderate Buy consensus rating, with a forecasted upside potential of approximately 21.13%. Despite their unique qualities and high dividend yields, DEA and PSTL trade at reasonable valuations, with DEA at around 11.5x projected FFO and PSTL at 16.2x. These factors position them as promising investments, offering safety without overpaying in the current uncertain environment (Sismanis, 2022).

RISK ASSESSMENT

- **Market Risks**

Identifying potential market risks is crucial in evaluating the investment potential of Government REITs such as DEA and PSTL. While DEA and PSTL have shown resilience with high dividend yields and reasonable valuations, other REIT types carry higher inherent risks. The commercial real estate landscape underwent significant changes during the COVID-19 pandemic, leading to a lasting impact on market dynamics. Despite the pandemic waning, the recovery of commercial real estate properties, especially those catering to office space, has been sluggish due to continued soft demand. The prevalence of hybrid working models further challenges the prospects of office spaces, while industrial properties face uncertainty with rising interest rates and a slowing economy. Given these circumstances, DEA and PSTL stand out as interesting REITs because they focus on a well-known, high-quality tenant, the U.S. government.

- **Interest Rate Sensitivity**

One critical aspect of risk assessment for Government REITs involves understanding their sensitivity to changes in interest rates. DEA and PSTL's unique advantages lie in serving as landlords to mission-critical U.S. Federal Agencies and the USPS, respectively. This specialized focus provides them with a stronghold against typical market risks. The unparalleled creditworthiness of the U.S. government serves as a robust moat for DEA and PSTL, differentiating them from ordinary REITs. The U.S. government, widely recognized as the most trustworthy global creditor, ensures that rental payments are secure, even for mission-critical properties housing vital agencies. The ability of the government to print money to meet its obligations eliminates counterparty risk and rent collection issues, offering a significant advantage over ordinary REITs facing these challenges.

Moreover, the essential nature of the agencies leased by DEA and PSTL ensures their continuous existence, contributing to a stable income stream. With a 100% occupancy ratio since its public listing and a lengthy weighted average lease term of 19.6 years, DEA provides investors with an unparalleled margin of safety. PSTL, with a 99.7% occupancy rate and a slightly shorter weighted average lease term, still offers secured cash flows over the medium term.

Despite the uncertain market environment, DEA and PSTL emerge as unique and promising investments. Their risk profiles are notably reduced compared to ordinary REITs, given their exclusive focus on high-quality government tenants, resulting in reliable yields. The reasonable valuations of these REITs trade further enhance their attractiveness to investors seeking safety without overpaying in the current economic landscape (Sismanis, 2022).

PERFORMANCE OF GOVERNMENT REITS ACROSS ECONOMIC CYCLES

REITs specializing in government properties have demonstrated resilience across various economic cycles. This stability is particularly evident in late-cycle periods, providing investors with a reliable defense against market challenges. Historical data since 1991 indicates that U.S. REITs have consistently outperformed the S&P 500 by over 7% annually during late-cycle phases. This outperformance extends to periods of recession, emphasizing the value of defensive, lease-based revenues and high dividend yields amid heightened uncertainty (Bohjalian, 2019):

Key Insights:

1. Late-Cycle Resilience

U.S. REITs have shown a remarkable ability to weather market uncertainties in late-cycle phases. The annualized total return data from 1991 to 2018 illustrates that while the S&P 500 experienced downturns, U.S. REITs demonstrated positive returns, highlighting their defensive characteristics.

2. Recent Market Shift

The narrative around REITs has shifted, especially towards the end of 2018. As global growth slowed and liquidity tightened, U.S. REITs outperformed broad equities, experiencing a smaller drawdown (–6.7%) compared to the S&P 500 (–13.5%). This shift in performance suggests a potential change in market leadership.

3. Factors Driving Late-Cycle Outperformance

Several factors contribute to the historical outperformance of REITs in late-cycle environments:

- **Lease-Based Revenues**: REITs often have predictable, lease-based revenues, providing consistent earnings growth. This stability is particularly evident in the face of economic downturns.
- **Dividend Payments**: REITs historically pay attractive dividends, offering investors a head start on returns, especially in low-growth environments. Regulatory requirements mandate U.S. REITs to distribute at least 90% of taxable income to shareholders.
- **Interest Rate Dynamics**: Slower economic growth tends to alleviate pressure from rising interest rates. The Federal Reserve's dovish stance and a potential peak in economic growth contribute to a favorable environment for REITs.

4. Favorable Backdrop for Real Estate

The overall backdrop for real estate, as of 2019, is positive for REITs. Healthy fundamentals, strong balance sheets, low correlations with other asset classes, and attractive valuations contribute to the appeal of REIT investments.

5. Support from Private Investment Demand

Private real estate funds are sitting on a record $300 billion in uninvested capital, looking to acquire assets similar to those owned by REITs. This demand may act as a supportive factor for REIT valuations. In conclusion, Government REITs' historical performance and characteristics suggest they can be robust investment options, especially in late-cycle phases, providing investors with a balance of stability, income, and potential for attractive returns.

Tips for Successful Government REIT Investing

Due Diligence and Research

- Conducting Thorough Research

Before investing in Government REITs, it is imperative to conduct comprehensive research. Investors should delve into the unique aspects of Government REITs, understanding their market positions, tenant profiles, and lease structures. Examining financial health indicators and historical performance metrics can provide valuable insights into these REITs' stability and potential returns.

- Staying Informed

Staying updated on market and industry news is crucial for Government REIT investors. Market dynamics can change rapidly, impacting the performance of real estate assets. Regularly monitoring news related to government policies, economic trends, and the overall real estate market ensures that investors can make informed decisions based on the latest information.

Risk Management

- Diversification Techniques

Diversification is a key risk management strategy. Investors should explore diversifying their Government REIT investments across different REITs, sectors, or geographic regions. This helps mitigate the impact of localized economic challenges or sector-specific issues on the overall portfolio.

- Setting Realistic Expectations

Managing expectations is vital in Government REIT investing. While these REITs offer stability, it is essential to understand that returns may vary. Setting realistic expectations based on historical performance, market conditions, and economic outlook can help investors navigate fluctuations in the market.

Long-Term vs. Short-Term Investment

- Long-Term Investment Benefits

Holding Government REITs for the long term provides several advantages. Investors can benefit from stable rental income, potential property appreciation, and the compounding effect of reinvested dividends. Long-term investments align well with the inherent stability offered by Government REITs, making them suitable for investors with a strategic, patient approach.

- Short-Term Strategies

Strategic approaches such as tactical allocation or opportunistic buying/selling may be considered for investors with short-term goals. However, it is essential to recognize that Government REITs are inherently geared towards stability, and short-term strategies should align with the investor's overall risk tolerance and objectives.

SECTION 3: CASE STUDIES IN GOVERNMENT REIT SUCCESS

REAL-LIFE SUCCESS STORIES

- Notable Government REIT Successes

Exploring real-life success stories of Government REITs, such as PSTL and DEA, highlights the resilience and stability these investments can bring. These case studies serve as tangible examples of how Government REITs, with their exclusive focus on reliable government tenants, can deliver consistent returns and weather market uncertainties.

- Key Takeaways from Case Studies

Analyzing these success stories provides valuable lessons for investors. Key takeaways include

- the importance of having mission-critical government agencies as tenants,
- the advantages of long-term lease agreements and
- the resilience offered by Government REITs in the face of economic challenges.

Investors can gain insights into replicable strategies that contribute to the success of their own Government REIT investments. The journey through Government REITs unfolds as a strategic odyssey, guiding investors through the multifaceted terrain of real estate investments, combining stability, income, and the potential for attractive returns.

SUMMARY

In this comprehensive exploration, we have delved into Government REITs' often underappreciated asset class and their pivotal role in shaping a diversified and resilient investment landscape. The absence of REITs in client portfolios prompts a critical inquiry, considering that commercial real estate constitutes 16% of U.S. investments. We explored how Government REITs, particularly exemplified by PSTL and DEA, provide stability and income, shielded from market concerns, and backed by the unmatched creditworthiness of the U.S. government.

The narrative unfolds as a strategic odyssey, guiding investors, financial professionals, and enthusiasts through the multifaceted terrain of real estate investments. We have covered key features and benefits, appropriate allocation strategies, and the consensus among financial advisors regarding the enduring fundamentals of Government REITs. Insights from Morningstar's research and real-world success stories underscore the resilience and longevity of Government REITs.

The chapter also provides a detailed breakdown of tax characteristics associated with Government REIT distributions, emphasizing transparency and accountability. The assessment of investment potential includes analyzing the financial health, portfolio composition, and unique advantages of Government REITs like DEA and PSTL. Risk assessment explores market risks and interest rate sensitivity, highlighting the reduced risk profiles of DEA and PSTL compared to ordinary REITs. The performance of Government REITs across economic cycles, especially their resilience in late-cycle phases, adds to their appeal for investors seeking stability, income, and potential returns.

Tips for successful Government REIT investing encompass thorough research, staying informed, risk management through diversification, and setting realistic expectations. The chapter concludes with case studies of real-life successes exemplified by PSTL and DEA, providing valuable lessons and insights for investors.

Empowered with this knowledge, your journey to REIT mastery is poised for success. The strategic odyssey through Government REITs combines stability, income, and the potential for attractive returns, guiding you through the multifaceted terrain of real estate investments. As you embark on this journey, in the next chapter, the lessons learned from the comprehensive insights will empower you to achieve financial success in the dynamic realm of investment portfolios.

CHAPTER 9

NAVIGATING THE FUTURE OF COMMERCIAL REITS

REAL ESTATE, long regarded as the bedrock of prosperity for the world's affluent, is an ever-evolving landscape brimming with diverse opportunities. As this dynamic realm undergoes continuous meta-morphosis, a nuanced understanding of its intricate dance becomes increasingly pivotal. In this exploration, we dive deep into the currents shaping the contemporary real estate investment scene, uncovering the resurgence of REITs, the revolutionary impact of crowdfunding, the irresistible allure of the Sunbelt, the steadfast rise of multifamily real estate, and the intriguing glimpse into the future with personalized REITs (DealEstate.Ai, 2023):

- **The Remarkable Resurgence of REITs**

With their roots dating back to 1960, REITs have emerged as fundamental players in the investment universe. Today, we witness a significant resurgence, with REITs flexing their financial muscle by raising an impressive $178.2 billion in equity capital in the first half of 2023 alone—a staggering leap of 52% from the previous year. Unraveling the factors propelling this REIT renaissance, we explore the quest for stable income, the dynamics of diversification, and the role of REITs as a safeguard against inflation.

- **A New Dawn in Real Estate Investment**

The landscape of real estate investment undergoes a paradigm shift with the advent of crowdfunding—a modern phenomenon rooted in traditional collective investment practices. In 2022, the U.S. crowdfunding realm hit the $10.4 billion mark, marking a transformative force in the industry. We dissect the game-changing aspects of crowdfunding, including its role in democratizing investment, providing diverse opportunities on a global scale, and ushering in unparalleled transparency through digital advancements.

- **The Irresistible Charm of the Sunbelt**

In the vast expanse of real estate, the Sunbelt region emerges as a focal point of unprecedented popularity, accounting for a staggering 42% of commercial real estate deals in 2023. We uncover the driving forces behind this surge, exploring demographic shifts, economic factors, and the allure of a lower cost of living that positions Sunbelt cities as increasingly attractive alternatives to traditional hubs.

- **The Steadfast Rise of Multifamily Real Estate**

July 2023 marks not just an anomaly but a continuation of the consistent growth witnessed by the multifamily property segment. We delve into the rationale behind this sustained boom, examining the efficiency of managing multifamily units, the appeal of steady revenue streams, and the potential for value addition through innovative transformations.

- **A Glimpse into the Future?**

As innovation becomes the driving force in real estate, we explore the nascent concept of personalized REITs. At the forefront, platforms aim to align investments with individual financial dreams and goals. This chapter ventures into the potential paradigm shift where crafting portfolios transcends traditional boundaries, offering a personalized investment experience that caters to the unique aspirations of investors.

Section 1: PropTech and Real Estate

The real estate industry, known for its historical conservatism, is undergoing a paradigm shift propelled by technological advancements. Proptech, a term encompassing technology-driven innovations in real estate, is gaining momentum and reshaping the investment and interaction dynamics within the industry. This section explores how Proptech is revolutionizing real estate, particularly its integration into Commercial REITs to elevate efficiency and enhance the tenant experience. Additionally, we dive into compelling case studies that illuminate successful proptech implementations in the realm of commercial real estate (Uche, 2023):

Subsection 1.1: Online Property Marketplaces

A significant stride made by proptech in real estate investing is the emergence of online property marketplaces. These platforms seamlessly connect buyers, sellers, and investors, revolutionizing the search, analysis, and investment processes. The convenience of remotely accessing a vast inventory of properties, reviewing detailed information, comparing prices, and even conducting virtual property tours has heightened transparency and efficiency and expanded investment opportunities beyond geographical constraints.

Subsection 1.2: Real Estate Data and Analytics

Proptech's impact extends to the analytical realm, transforming investors' evaluation of potential opportunities. Real estate data and analytics platforms provide investors comprehensive insights and market trends, empowering data-driven decision-making. By employing advanced algorithms and machine learning, these platforms analyze extensive data sets, including property values, rental yields, market demand, and demographic information, enabling investors to make informed choices, optimize portfolios, and maximize returns.

Subsection 1.3: Crowdfunding and Fractional Ownership

Proptech has democratized real estate investing through crowdfunding and fractional ownership models. These platforms enable multiple investors to pool resources and invest in high-value properties previously inaccessible to individuals. Crowdfunding facilitates diverse investment opportunities, spreading risk across various real estate projects, while fractional ownership platforms offer flexibility by allowing investors to purchase a fraction of a property, enhancing liquidity in managing portfolios.

Subsection 1.4: Smart Building Management

In the Internet of Things (IoT) era, smart building management systems stand out as a game-changer in real estate. Leveraging interconnected devices and sensors, these systems optimize energy efficiency, bolster security, and elevate tenant experiences. For real estate investors, adopting smart building technologies reduces operating costs, increases property value, and improves tenant retention rates. Remote monitoring and control capabilities empower investors to enhance operational efficiency and sustainability across various building systems.

Subsection 1.5: Blockchain and Smart Contracts

Blockchain technology holds transformative potential for real estate transactions, offering secure, transparent, and tamper-proof property ownership and transaction records. Blockchain-based platforms streamline purchase and sale processes, eliminate intermediaries, and reduce transaction costs. Powered by blockchain, smart contracts automate and enforce contract terms, ensuring trust and efficiency in real estate transactions. This technology opens doors to fractional ownership, tokenization of assets, and innovative investment models like blockchain-based REITs.

SECTION 2: SUSTAINABLE AND RESPONSIBLE INVESTING

Exploring the Ascendance of Sustainability in REITs

- Sustainability has become a pivotal consideration in recent years, underscoring its significance by the pressing environmental and social challenges facing the world. This is particularly relevant in commercial REITs, where adopting sustainable practices has evolved from a trend to a necessity (Tayf Egypt, 2023).

Defining Sustainable Development in Real Estate

- Sustainable development in real estate entails the construction of buildings designed to minimize their adverse impact on the environment, prioritize energy efficiency, and act responsibly within the surrounding ecosystem. This section dives into the role of sustainable development in commercial real estate investment, emphasizing why investors should prioritize sustainable practices in their decision-making.

Understanding Sustainable Development:

- Sustainable development is a philosophy centered on meeting present needs without compromising the ability of future generations to meet their own requirements. It involves a delicate balance of economic, social, and environmental considerations to ensure that development remains sustainable in the long term. In the context of commercial REITs, sustainable development translates to investments in properties that are not only economically viable but also environmentally and socially responsible.

- Importance of Sustainable Development in Commercial Real Estate Investment:
- Several compelling reasons underscore the importance of sustainable development in commercial real estate investment:

Risk Management:

- Sustainable properties can act as a risk management strategy, particularly regarding energy efficiency. Such properties tend to have lower operating costs, providing protection against rising energy prices.
- Locations with excellent access to public transportation enhance resilience in the face of oil price shocks.

Regulatory Compliance:

- Investing in sustainable properties ensures compliance with evolving environmental and social regulations globally.
- Stringent regulations on issues like energy efficiency and carbon emissions make sustainable properties less prone to regulatory risks.

Increased Property Value:

- Sustainable properties, such as energy-efficient buildings, appeal to tenants willing to pay higher rents for lower operating costs.
- Properties strategically located with good access to public transportation also attract tenants willing to pay a premium to avoid commuting inconveniences.

Enhanced Reputation:

- Investing in sustainable properties enhances an investor's reputation by demonstrating a commitment to environmental and social responsibility.
- This commitment can attract socially conscious tenants and investors, positively influencing an investor's standing in the market.

Incorporating Sustainable Development into Investment Decisions:

- Investors can seamlessly incorporate sustainable development into their investment decisions through several key practices.

Conducting Due Diligence:

- Prioritize sustainability credentials by evaluating factors such as energy efficiency, carbon footprint, waste management, and accessibility.

Engaging with Stakeholders:

- Engage with stakeholders, including tenants, local communities, and regulators, to understand sustainability priorities and concerns.
- Identify opportunities to create value through sustainable development based on stakeholder input.

Setting Sustainability Targets:

- Set sustainability targets for investment properties, such as reducing energy consumption or waste generation.
- Regularly monitor progress toward sustainability goals and identify areas for improvement.

Measuring and Reporting Sustainability Performance:

- Implement measures to assess and report on the sustainability performance of investment properties.
- Demonstrate commitment to sustainability and social responsibility, identifying opportunities for continuous improvement.

SECTION 3: FUTURE SECTORS AND OPPORTUNITIES

- **Navigating the Shifting Landscape of Commercial Real Estate (CRE) Investment**

Insights from Industry Experts: Jim Garman, Kristin Kuney, and Marco Willner (Garman et al., 2023). The commercial real estate (CRE) sector finds itself during a cyclical downturn marked by notable disparities in asset prices, regional dynamics, and property types. As investors grapple with reducing risk amidst areas of stress, intriguing opportunities are emerging across both public and private markets. The key to success lies in adeptly accessing and managing assets influenced by technological innovation, evolving demographics, and sustainability trends.

Adaptation to a New Paradigm:

- The CRE landscape is undergoing a transformation, influenced by higher interest rates, softer fundamentals, and a departure from the reliance on a continuous influx of capital. Changing work and spending patterns further contribute to supply and demand imbalances. While the U.S. office market has been a focal point, divergences between asset types and regions have become more pronounced. Opportunities arise from mismatches in property prices, long-term value potential, and the overarching trends of technology, demographics, and sustainability.

Caution Amidst Repositioning:

- As real estate assets undergo repricing and face a substantial wave of maturities exceeding $2 trillion over the next three years, caution prevails among investors. Commercial real estate deal activity has notably slowed, reflecting fundamental challenges, increased cost, and decreased credit availability. The balance of distress in the U.S. and a decline in CRE acquisitions across Europe signal a nuanced recovery trajectory, with uneven outcomes anticipated across regions.

Identifying Opportunities Amidst Challenges:

Offices: Flight to Quality

- Despite challenges in the office sector with curtailed leasing activity and downsizing, a 'flight-to-quality' trend is boosting prime office rents. Prime locations in major cities continue to attract tenants, while less-developed metros are witnessing growth.
- Sustainability considerations impact tenant choices, with a 'green premium' observed in occupiers' willingness to pay higher rents for environmentally certified buildings.

Retail: A Dynamic Landscape

- Retail faces significant disruption from e-commerce and pandemic-related rent losses. The resumption of international tourism and resilient consumer balance sheets offer some confidence.
- Trends in retail vary globally, with a shift in strategies and focus outside traditional urban cores. Grocery stores and mixed-use spaces gain importance, emphasizing adaptability for developers and a focus on prime assets for investors.

Rethinking the Right Side of Disruption

- Specific CRE sub-sectors driven by secular growth trends may prove more resilient. Data centers, industrial warehouses, and buildings aligned with demographic changes, such as senior and student housing, are highlighted. The international emergence of 5G, blockchain, and cloud computing presents significant opportunities for technology real estate. Data centers, in particular, exhibit resilience and strong demand, necessitating adaptation for future technological needs.

Industrial and E-Commerce: Meeting Evolving Demand

- E-commerce is a driving force behind robust demand for industrial and logistics properties. Automation and robotics play a crucial role, with occupiers willing to pay a premium for modern warehouses. The trend towards onshoring supply chains further supports demand in select industrial markets. Early recognition of these evolutions can provide an advantage in securing high-quality assets in prime locations.

Mind the Gaps: Public vs. Private Valuations

- Public REITs have adjusted to higher interest rates and slower growth, experiencing valuations down from the peak. While underperforming public markets, the private market has seen more muted adjustments. The public vs. private valuation gap is scrutinized, with questions about sustainability. History suggests a potential decline in private market valuations to align with public prices, emphasizing the importance of rigorous asset analysis.

Looking Ahead: Key Themes and Strategies:

- Slowing inflation, potential rate reductions, and tighter credit spreads are anticipated to influence CRE's fundamental health in the coming quarters.
- Interest rate stabilization, potential disposals, and the ability to pass on high inflation to tenants are identified as catalysts that may spur transaction volumes.
- Sector and regional divergence presents challenges and opportunities, emphasizing the need for active investment in high-quality assets aligned with technological innovation, shifting demographics, and sustainability trends. A tailored approach is crucial in this dynamic market, as one size does not fit all.

SUMMARY

In this chapter, we embark on a journey through the resurging realms of real estate, unveiling the resurgence of REITs and their pivotal role as financial powerhouses. With a substantial 52% increase, REITs raised a staggering $178.2 billion in the first half of 2023, emphasizing their significance in providing stable income, diversification, and a hedge against inflation. The narrative then transitions to the dawn of a new era in real estate investment, marked by the transformative force of crowdfunding. Exploring the democratization of investment, the chapter dives into the $10.4 billion U.S. crowdfunding landscape of 2022, highlighting its role in providing diverse global opportunities and ushering in transparency through digital advancements.

The irresistible charm of the Sunbelt region takes center stage, constituting 42% of commercial real estate deals in 2023. Demographic shifts, economic factors, and a lower cost of living position Sunbelt cities as attractive alternatives to traditional hubs, inviting investors to explore the unique opportunities they offer. The steadfast rise of multifamily real estate is examined, showcasing its consistent growth. The chapter unravels the efficiency of managing multifamily units, the allure of steady revenue streams, and the potential for value addition through innovative transformations.

A glimpse into the future is offered through the exploration of personalized REITs, envisioning a paradigm shift where portfolio crafting transcends traditional boundaries. This forward-looking concept caters to the unique aspirations of investors, providing a personalized investment experience. As we explore the realm of Proptech and its transformative impact on real estate, case studies illustrate successful implementations, particularly within Commercial REITs. The integration of technology elevates efficiency and enhances tenant experiences, ushering in a new era in real estate dynamics.

Shifting gears, the chapter then explores sustainable and responsible investing, defining sustainable development in commercial real estate. It underscores the importance of balancing economic, social, and environmental considerations, showcasing how sustainable practices act as risk management strategies, ensure regulatory compliance, and enhance property value and reputation. The chapter concludes with a forward-looking gaze into future sectors and opportunities in CRE. Industry experts guide us through the cyclical downturn, emphasizing the potential in areas influenced by technological innovation, shifting demographics, and sustainability trends. Diverse opportunities emerge in offices, retail, technology real estate, industrial, and e-commerce sectors. Armed with insights into REIT resurgence, crowdfunding dynamics, regional hotspots, and future landscapes. In the next chapter, you will be empowered to embark on a path toward financial success in the dynamic world of real estate investment.

CHAPTER 10

YOUR JOURNEY TO REIT MASTERY

THIS SECTION INVITES professionals to explore the dynamic realm of REITs as a promising pathway within the real estate industry. It highlights the diverse opportunities available, catering to individuals aspiring to be real estate agents or investment analysts. The chapter promises a comprehensive journey through career options, key insights, goal-setting, and actions for achieving financial independence and stability. It acknowledges both the benefits and potential challenges associated with pursuing a career in real estate investment through REITs (Finance Grub, 2023):

1. Understanding REITs:

REITs simplify real estate investment by allowing professionals to participate without the complexities of direct ownership. They offer a unique investment avenue within the real estate sector, providing the benefits of property ownership without the burdens of managing individual properties. A key aspect of REITs is their commitment to distributing taxable income to shareholders as dividends, making them an appealing choice for investors seeking consistent income streams. By pooling resources from various investors, REITs create diversified property portfolios, reducing individual risks and leveraging economies of scale. In essence, REITs serve as a bridge between traditional real estate and stock market investments, offering simplicity, liquidity, and diversification. They enable investors to ride the waves of real estate growth and income potential, presenting an innovative and dynamic approach to building wealth in the ever-evolving real estate landscape.

2. Disadvantages of a REIT Career:

While a career in REITs offers numerous rewards, it's essential to consider potential drawbacks, including market swings, dependency on real estate performance, dividend pressure, and high competition.

3. Largest REITs in North America:

Some of the biggest REITs are in North America, like Prologis (PLD) and American Tower (AMT).

4. Highest-Paying Jobs in Real Investment Trusts:

The highest-paying jobs in REITs typically include roles in senior management or those managing large portfolios. Salaries vary based on factors like company size, location, and individual experience. Even entry-level REIT positions can offer competitive salaries, starting around $70,000 annually.

5. Job Opportunities in REITs:

According to indeed.com, there are over 6,000 REIT job openings in the United States, covering roles such as analyst, property manager, developer, financier, marketer, and sales.

- Real Estate Agent
- Investment Analyst
- Property Manager
- Investor Relations Manager

6. Starting a Career in REITs:

Embarking on a career in REITs requires a blend of education, skills, networking, and relevant experience. Here is a guide to help set you on the path to success in the REIT domain:

- Get Suitable Education
- Immerse in Financial Insights
- Glean Real Estate Details
- Harvest Professional Expertise
- Contemplate Advanced Education
- Forge Connections
- Peek into REIT Enclaves
- Seize REIT Avenues
- Showcase Your Prowess

7. Career Options in REITs:

Within the realm of REITs, various career options await, including:

- Insight into Real Estate Trends and Market Wisdom
- Networking and Resources
- Realm of Specialization
- Dynamic and Innovative Environment
- Shaping the Real Estate Landscape
- Embracing Diverse Real Estate Assets
- Investment Prospects

8. Evaluating REITs as a Career Path:

Deciding whether a career in REITs is a good fit depends on personal aspirations, career objectives, and skills. As you contemplate a career in REITs, consider factors such as those passionate about real estate and finance. REITs offer a rewarding niche with a range of career possibilities, market insight, stable remuneration, and a trajectory toward growth.

- Equity Real Estate Investment Trusts
- Mortgage Real Estate Investment Trusts
- Hybrid Real Estate Investment Trusts
- Residential Real Estate Investment Trusts
- Commercial Real Estate Investment Trusts
- Retail Real Estate Investment Trusts
- Industrial Real Estate Investment Trusts
- Healthcare Real Estate Investment Trusts
- Lodging Real Estate Investment Trusts
- Data Center Real Estate Investment Trusts

9. Exploring Different Types of REITs:

REITs come in various types based on their investments and the nature of the real estate assets they manage. Some major types include Understanding these subgenres, which can assist investors in making informed choices or professionals in charting a career path aligned with their expertise and interests.

Key Takeaways

- **Subsection 1: Overview of REITs**

This section provides a comprehensive recap of REITs, encompassing key takeaways, advantages, debunking myths, legal frameworks, recent trends, case studies, and investment strategies. This analysis aims to equip you with a deep understanding of REITs, guiding you toward informed investment decisions.

In understanding the fundamental concept of REITs, these entities emerge as the bridge between traditional real estate and stock market investments. Commercial REITs, a blend of tangibility and fluidity, offer investors the benefits of property ownership without the associated hassles. This chapter emphasized the historical development of REITs, stemming from a vision in 1960 to democratize commercial real estate investments globally. Consolidating investor capital allows individuals to benefit from real estate ventures without direct property management. Moving forward, comparing direct property ownership with REITs, landlords may experience leverage benefits and high returns, but it demands significant hands-on management. On the other hand, REITs offer simplicity, diversification, and liquidity but may need more rapid growth of direct real estate due to distribution requirements.

- **Subsection 2: Advantages of REITs**

The second section highlights the advantages of REITs, positioning them as a bridge between commercial real estate and publicly traded stocks. Historical performance, income distribution mandates, and unique perks make REITs popular among investors.

- **Subsection 3: Debunking Myths around REITs**

The narrative in Section 3 uncovers the sector's complexities, dispelling misconceptions about capital requirements, risk levels, and the necessity of prior experience. Potential investors are encouraged to explore diverse opportunities within the REIT landscape.

- **Subsection 4: Legal Frameworks and Global Trends**

The fourth section explores legal frameworks globally, focusing on Malta's adoption of a REIT framework. Associations related to REITs are discussed, offering valuable resources and support.

- **Subsection 5: Recent Trends**

Section 5 discusses recent trends, emphasizing REITs' growing significance, economic impact, global adoption, and the importance of effective valuation.

- **Subsection 6: Case Study and Foundation for Investment**

In the sixth section, a deep dive into the world of Commercial REITs elucidates their history, evolution, advantages, and the broader ecosystem that supports and regulates them. This chapter sets the foundation for maximizing returns and mitigating risks in REITs. Recognizing the importance of diversification, the chapter emphasizes the potential dangers of concentrating investments in a single sector, advocating for diversification across sectors, geographies, and property types.

- **Subsection 7: Crafting a Robust REIT Investment Strategy**

The seventh section dives into the practical aspects of designing a robust REIT investment plan. Recognizing the landscape of REITs as a bridge between the concrete world of real estate and the dynamic realm of stock markets, the chapter emphasizes the potential benefits of both stability and the thrill of market dynamics.

- **Subsection 8: Selecting REITs with Confidence**

Section 8 explores the specifics of REIT selection, equipping readers with the expertise to make informed decisions and maximize their investment potential. The historical role of real estate, the simplicity of REITs, and potential advantages are highlighted. Meticulous evaluation of fundamentals, management, and portfolio diversity is emphasized.

- **Subsection 9: Lessons from REIT Veterans**

Section 9 engages in conversations with REIT veterans, offering insights and experiences from seasoned investors. These individuals have navigated the REIT landscape, faced its challenges, and reaped its rewards. Their wisdom provides a unique perspective on real estate investments through REITs.

- **Subsection 10: Avoiding Pitfalls in REIT Investments**

Section 10 comprehensively explores REITs, outlining the challenges and pitfalls associated with mastering the art of REIT investments in 2023. This section discusses crucial components of learning from past mistakes, emphasizing due diligence, and avoiding overleveraging.

- **Subsection 11: Government REITs**

Section 11 explored the often-overlooked realm of Government REITs, illuminating their pivotal role in cultivating a diversified and resilient investment landscape. The inquiry into the absence of REITs in client portfolios, juxtaposed with the substantial 16% representation of commercial real estate in U.S. investments, sets the stage. Government REITs, epitomized by PSTL and DEA, emerge as stalwarts, providing stability and income shielded from market concerns, backed by the unparalleled creditworthiness of the U.S. government. The narrative unfolds as a strategic odyssey, guiding investors and financial professionals through the multifaceted terrain of real estate investments. This subsection encapsulates key aspects, including allocation strategies, insights from Morningstar, tax characteristics, investment potential assessment, risk analysis, and the performance of Government REITs across economic cycles. It concludes with actionable tips for successful Government REIT investing and real-life case studies exemplified by PSTL and DEA. Empowered with this knowledge, you are poised for success in your journey to REIT mastery, combining stability, income, and the potential for attractive returns in the dynamic realm of investment portfolios.

- **Subsection 12: Resurgence and Future Trends**

The final section embarks on a journey through the resurging realms of real estate, unveiling the resurgence of REITs and their pivotal role as financial powerhouses. With a substantial increase in REIT capital raising, the report explores the transformative force of crowdfunding, regional hotspots, and future trends in Commercial Real Estate (CRE).

SUMMARY

In this enlightening chapter, we embarked on a journey into the dynamic realm of REITs, offering a comprehensive exploration of the career opportunities and key considerations within this thriving industry. Beginning with an understanding of REITs as entities that own, operate, and finance income-generating real estate properties, the chapter emphasizes their appeal to professionals seeking diverse opportunities in real estate investment without the complexities of direct ownership. Diving into the various REIT types, such as equity, mortgage, hybrid, residential, commercial, and more, the chapter provides insights for individuals to align their career paths with their expertise and interests. Aspiring to bridge the gap between traditional real estate and stock market investments, the narrative unfolds, covering factors influencing a career in REITs, diverse roles available, and practical steps to initiate a successful journey. The chapter provides a comprehensive guide for those considering a career in this dynamic field by offering a glimpse into job opportunities, the highest-paying roles, and the largest REITs in North America. It also candidly addresses potential disadvantages, ensuring a balanced perspective. Concluding with key takeaways, the chapter serves as a valuable resource, equipping readers with a deep understanding of REITs for informed decision-making in both career and investment pursuits.

CONCLUSION

In closing, this book on REITs comprehensively explores an exciting and dynamic realm within the real estate industry. Throughout the chapters, we have dived into the fundamental concept of REITs, positioning them as a bridge between traditional real estate and the stock market. This journey has unfolded, offering a nuanced understanding of the advantages, dispelling myths, exploring legal frameworks and global trends, and providing insights into recent developments and case studies.

The historical development of REITs, stemming from a vision in 1960 to democratize commercial real estate investments globally, has laid the foundation for individuals to benefit from real estate ventures without the burden of direct property management. The comparison between direct property ownership and REITs underscores the trade-offs between hands-on management and the simplicity, diversification, and liquidity REITs offer.

Advancing through the chapters, I have highlighted the advantages of REITs as a bridge between commercial real estate and publicly traded stocks, emphasizing historical performance, income distribution mandates, and unique perks that make REITs popular among investors. The narrative has also worked to dispel misconceptions about capital requirements, risk levels, and the necessity of prior experience, encouraging potential investors to explore diverse opportunities within the REIT landscape.

Legal frameworks, global trends, recent developments, and a deep dive into commercial REITs have provided a robust foundation for understanding and navigating the REIT landscape. The importance of crafting a powerful REIT investment strategy, selecting REITs with confidence, and drawing lessons from seasoned REIT veterans further contribute to the comprehensive knowledge shared in this book.

The exploration of Government REITs in Section 11 sheds light on an often-overlooked realm, showcasing their pivotal role in cultivating a diversified and resilient investment landscape. Government REITs, exemplified by PSTL and DEA, emerge as stalwarts, providing stability and income shielded from market concerns, backed by the unparalleled creditworthiness of the U.S. government. This strategic odyssey, rich in insights from Morningstar, allocation strategies, tax characteristics, and real-life case studies, equips readers for success in their journey to REIT mastery.

As we conclude, the resurgence and future trends in REITs are highlighted, underlining the transformative force of crowdfunding, regional hotspots, and the evolving landscape of CRE. The key takeaway is that you are now armed with a powerful tool—the knowledge and insights shared in this book. It is time to turn these pages into real-world success and make your real estate investment dreams a reality.

Your journey to REIT mastery is marked by stability, income, and the potential for attractive returns in the dynamic realm of investment portfolios. As you embark on this journey, consider sharing your thoughts on the book through a review. Your feedback is invaluable, and by sharing your insights, you contribute to the collective knowledge and success of the REIT community.

Thank you for joining us on this exploration of REITs. May your ventures be prosperous and your investments yield the returns you envision. Here is to your success in the dynamic world of real estate investments!

Scan the QR code to leave your review!

Review Link!

GLOSSARY

Commercial Real Estate: Income-generating real estate used for business purposes, such as office buildings, retail spaces, and industrial facilities.

Commercial Real Estate Investment: Investing in income-generating properties used for business purposes.

Creditworthiness: The assessment of a person's or entity's ability to fulfill financial obligations based on credit history and financial stability.

Crowdfunding: A method of raising capital by gathering small amounts of money from a large number of people often facilitated through online platforms.

Data Center Real Estate Investment Trusts: REITs that own and operate data center facilities.

Dividends: Distributions disbursed by a company to its shareholders using its earnings.

Due Diligence: The process of thorough research and analysis conducted before making business decisions, such as investing in REITs.

Economies of Scale: The cost advantages that result from increased production or operational efficiency.

Equity Real Estate Investment Trusts: REITs primarily possessing and managing revenue-generating real estate assets.

Financial Independence: Achieving a state where an individual's assets generate enough income to cover living expenses.

Healthcare Real Estate Investment Trusts: REITs that focus on healthcare-related properties, such as hospitals and medical office buildings.

Industrial Real Estate Investment Trusts: REITs that possess and manage industrial assets, such as warehouses and distribution centers.

Investment Analyst: A professional who analyzes financial data and market trends to provide investment recommendations.

Investor Relations Manager: A professional responsible for managing communications between a company and its investors.

Lodging Real Estate Investment Trusts: REITs specializing in lodging and hospitality properties, such as hotels and resorts.

Market Cap (Market Capitalization): The total value of a company's outstanding shares of stock, calculated by multiplying the share price by the number of shares.

Portfolio: A collection of financial assets, such as stocks, bonds, and real estate, held by an individual or entity.

Property Manager: An expert tasked with overseeing and upkeeping real estate holdings on behalf of the property owner.

Real Estate Agent: A certified professional who acts on behalf of buyers or sellers during real estate transactions.

Residential Real Estate Investment Trusts: REITs that focus on residential properties, such as apartment complexes and housing developments.

Retail Real Estate Investment Trusts: REITs specializing in retail properties, such as shopping malls and retail outlets.

Senior Management: Executives with high-level responsibilities in a company, often involved in decision-making and strategic planning.

Tax Characteristics: The tax-related attributes of an investment, including how income and gains are taxed.

REFERENCES

Aamer, Z. bin. (n.d.). *Analyzing a REIT for contribution or investment: key performance indicators.* CIEL. https://www.cielam.com/insights/analyzing-a-reit-for-contribu tion-or-investment-key-performance-indicators

Are REITs underrepresented in your clients' portfolios? (n.d.). Nareit. https://www.reit.com/ nareit/advocacy/investor-outreach/resources-financial-advisors?gad_source=1& gclid=CjwKCAiAjfyqBhAsEiwA-UdzJCZe_IPhUYwjLdtBCqgqNBuSsXs21xm_SyyoFyFw93USX8lmSyDk8RoCwa IQAvD_BwE

Ashworth, W. (2023, May 24). *5 types of REITs and how to Invest in them.* Investopedia. https://www.investopedia.com/articles/mortgages-real-estate/10/real-estate-invest ment-trust-reit.asp

Askola, J. (2023, October 3). *5 REITs that are overleveraged.* Seeking Alpha. https:// seekingalpha.com/article/4638157-5-reits-are-overleveraged

Batt, R., Appelbaum, E., & Katz, T. (2022). *The role of public REITs in financialization and industry restructuring* (No. 189). https://www.ineteconomics.org/uploads/papers/ WP_189-Batt-Appelbaum-Public-REITS-2.pdf

Beers, B. (2022, November 28). *How companies can reduce internal and external business risk.* Investopedia. https://www.investopedia.com/ask/answers/050115/how-can-companies-reduce-internal-and-external-business-risk.asp

Bitton, D. (2023, September 28). *REITs statistics: Key trends in 2023.* Door Loop. https:// www.doorloop.com/blog/reits-statistics#:~:text=

Bohjalian, T. (2019). *A REIT defense for the late cycle.* https://www.reit.com/sites/default/ files/media/PDFs/Research/C_S_REIT_Late_Cycle.pdf

Borchersen-Keto, S. (2014 June 20). *industry veteran says REITs remain low-volatility investments.* Nareit. https://www.reit.com/news/videos/industry-veteran-says-reits-remain-low-volatility-investments

Borchersen-Keto, S. (2022, November 17). *REIT portfolio managers assess key trends and issues for 2023.* Nareit. https://www.reit.com/news/reit-magazine/november-decem ber-2022/reit-portfolio-managers-assess-key-trends-and-issues-2023

brainyard. (n.d.). *Due diligence checklist.* https://www.netsuite.com/portal/assets/pdf/ brainyard-due-diligence-checklist.pdf

Brownlee, A. P. (2023, September 15). *Warren Buffett: be fearful when others are greedy.* Investopedia. https://www.investopedia.com/articles/investing/012116/warren-buffett-be-fearful-when-others-are-greedy.asp

CAGRFUNDS TEAM. (2018, May 31). *have you been taking hasty investment decisions?* CAGRFUNDS. https://www.cagrfunds.com/blog/have-you-been-taking-hasty-investment-decisions/

Chen, J. (2022, May 17). *investment strategy: ways to invest and factors to consider.* Investopedia. https://www.investopedia.com/terms/i/investmentstrategy.asp

Czar, J. (n.d.). *The largest database of properties & agents in Uganda.* Zillion Technologies Ltd. https://realestatedatabase.net/FindAHouse/Content.aspx?SelectedPageCode=8092&Title=Common+misconceptions+about+real+estate+agents+debunked.

DealEstate.Ai. (2023, August 22.). *the landscape of real estate investing: Exploring REITs, crowdfunding, and multifamily markets.* Linkedin. https://www.linkedin.com/pulse/landscape-real-estate-investing-exploring-reits-crowdfunding

Depersio, G. (2021, August 25). *Landlord vs. REITs: Pros and Cons.* Investopedia. https://www.investopedia.com/articles/mutual-funds/090516/landlord-vs-reits-pros-and-cons.asp#:~:text=

dvm360. (2022). *Real estate investment trust with majority veterinarian ownership is launched.* https://www.dvm360.com/view/real-estate-investment-trust-with-majority-veterinarian-ownership-is-launched

Easterly government properties announces tax characteristics of its 2022 Distributions. (2023, January 18). Easterly Government Properties Inc. https://ir.easterlyreit.com/news-releases/news-release-details/easterly-government-properties-announces-tax-characteristics-6

Everything Property. (2021, July 5). *Debunking common real estate myths.* https://everythingproperty.co.za/myth-debunking-common-real-estate-myths/

FasterCapital. (2023, October 15). *unveiling the past: analyzing dividend history for final dividend insights.* https://fastercapital.com/content/Unveiling-the-Past--Analyzing-Dividend-History-for-Final-Dividend-Insights.html#Uncovering-the-Significance-of-Dividend-History-Analysis

Feng, Z., Pattanapanchai, M., Price, S. M., & Sirmans, C. F. (2019). Geographic diversification in real estate investment trusts. *Real Estate Economics, 49*(2). https://doi.org/10.1111/1540-6229.12308

Finance Grub. (2023, August 20). *Is Real Estate Investment Trusts a Good Career Path?* Linkedin. https://www.linkedin.com/pulse/real-estate-investment-trusts-good-career-path-finance-grub

Fontinelle, A. (2023, April 13). *How To Adjust and Renew Your Portfolio.* Investopedia. https://www.investopedia.com/investing/how-renew-and-adjust-your-portfolio/#:~:text=

Garman, J., Kuney, K., & Willner, M. (2023, October 31). *COMMERCIAL REAL ESTATE: OPPORTUNITIES AMID DISLOCATION AND DISRUPTION.* Goldman Sachs. https://www.gsam.com/content/gsam/us/en/institutions/market-insights/gsam-insights/perspectives/2023/commercial-real-estate-opportunities-amid-dislocation-and-disruption.html#section-none

Ghosh, S. (2021, October 18). *Back 3 things you should keep in mind while investing in REITs.* Mint. https://www.livemint.com/money/personal-finance/3-things-you-should-keep-in-mind-while-investing-in-reits-11634572099076.html

Harper, D. R. (2022, June 2). *how to analyze REITs (Real Estate Investment Trusts).* Investopedia. https://www.investopedia.com/articles/04/030304.asp

Hayes, A. (2022, March 28). *Conservative Investing: Definition, Strategy Goals, Pros and*

Cons.   .Investopedia.   https://www.investopedia.com/terms/c/
conservativeinvesting.asp

Hayes, A. (2023, February 6). *Dividend Payout Ratio Definition, Formula, and Calculation.*
Investopedia. https://www.investopedia.com/terms/d/dividendpayoutratio.asp

Infina. (2023, February 23). *Case study: Diversified REIT portfolio delivers strong returns for
Dubai-based IT specialist.* Linkedin. https://www.linkedin.com/pulse/case-study-
diversified-reit-portfolio-delivers-strong-returns?trk=article-ssr-frontend-pulse_
more-articles_related-content-card

Investor.gov. (n.d.). *Real estate investment trust (REIT).* https://www.investor.gov/intro
duction-investing/investing-basics/glossary/real-estate-investment-trust-reit

LinkedIn Real Estate. (2023, March 10). *What are the common pitfalls and challenges of
investing in REITs?* Linkedin. https://www.linkedin.com/advice/0/what-common-
pitfalls-challenges-investing-reits-skills-real-estate

Mabece, Y. (2018). *A framework for mergers and acquisitions due diligence: Lessons from
selected REITs in South Africa* (Issue 863139) [University of Witwatersrand, Johannes-
burg, South Africa]. https://wiredspace.wits.ac.za/server/api/core/bitstreams/
361bbd8e-9630-49a1-8654-2fd69aba038b/content

MacBride, E. (2011, February 11). *Inside The Due Diligence That Uncovered Serious Questions About A REIT.* Forbes. https://www.forbes.com/sites/riabiz/2011/02/01/
inside-the-due-diligence-that-uncovered-serious-questions-about-a-reit/?sh=
40543083e3d1

*Million easterly government properties to issue $275, & notes private placement of senior unse-
cured.* (n.d.). Easterly Government Properties. https://www.sec.gov/Archives/edgar/
data/1622194/000156459019027204/dea-ex991_6.htm

Mind Tools Content Team. (n.d.). *SMART goals.* MindTools. https://www.mindtools.
com/a4wo118/smart-goals

Minogue, A. (2023). *Hedging your bets: Risk mitigation for investments. September 14.* AICPA
& CIMA. https://www.aicpa-cima.com/professional-insights/article/hedging-your-
bets-risk-mitigation-for-investments

Moskowitz, D. (2022, April 11). *What are the risks of real estate investment trusts (REITs)?*
Investopedia. https://www.investopedia.com/articles/investing/031915/what-are-
risks-reits.asp

Motley Fool Transcribing. (2023, July 28). *Digital realty trust (DLR) Q2 2023 earnings call
transcript.* The Motley Fool. https://www.fool.com/earnings/call-transcripts/2023/
07/28/digital-realty-trust-dlr-q2-2023-earnings-call-tra/

Nareit. (n.d.-a). *financial benefits of REITs.* https://www.reit.com/investing/financial-
benefits-reits#:~

Nareit. (n.d.-b). *History of REITs & real estate investing.* https://www.reit.com/what-reit/
history-reits

Nareit. (2017, June 22.). *Veteran REIT analyst says retail REITs well positioned for long term.*
https://www.reit.com/news/videos/veteran-reit-analyst-says-retail-reits-well-posi
tioned-long-term

Nareit Staff. (2019, May 15). *Postal Realty Trust, Inc. (NYSE: PSTL), a REIT that owns and
manages properties leased to the United States Postal Service (USPS), listed on the New York*

Stock   Exchange.   Nareit.   https://www.reit.com/news/articles/postal-realty-trust-lists-on-new-york-stock-exchange

Ndirangu, M. (2023, June 27). *Do not put all your eggs in one basket.* Linkedin. https://www.linkedin.com/pulse/do-put-all-your-eggs-one-basket-mercy-ndirangu#:~:text=

Okoro, C., & Ayaba, M. M. (2023). Research trends and directions on real estate investment trusts' performance risks. *Sustainability, 15*(6). https://doi.org/https://doi.org/10.3390/su15065436

Orzano, M., & Welling, J. (2017). The impact of rising interest rates on REITs. *S&P Dow Jones Indices.* https://www.spglobal.com/spdji/en/documents/research/the-impact-of-rising-interest-rates-on-reits.pdf

Pallardy, C. (2019, December 19). *Multi-billion dollar NYSE REIT veterans work to deploy $140m into the cannabis industry.* NEW CANNIBIS VENTURES. https://www.newcannabisventures.com/multi-billion-dollar-nyse-reit-veterans-work-to-deploy-140m-into-the-cannabis-industry-greenacreage/

Parker, P. M. (2019, September 4). *A comparison of the legal structures of REITs regimes implemented around the world.* CCLEX. https://www.cclex.com/publications/a-comparison-of-the-legal-structures-of-reits

Patterson, G. A. (2009). The relationship between REIT property types and economic risk factors. *ABD Journal, 1.* https://www.ship.edu/contentassets/569211b0c6f243808c3c64f54e816cd2/v1pattersonp15-p32.pdf

Pfeffer, T. (2008). *Performance of REITs a sector-and company based analysis of links and time lags between real estate market cycles, earnings, and pricing of REITs* [IRE BS]. https://epub.uni-regensburg.de/5849/6/49.pdf

Postal realty trust: Logistics delivering a 6.3% tax-advantaged yield. (2023, May 17). Ross Bowler. https://seekingalpha.com/article/4605352-postal-realty-trust-logistics-delivering-a-6-percent-tax-advantaged-yield

Probasco, J. (2023). *Declare your own financial independence day. July 3.* Investopedia. https://www.investopedia.com/financial-edge/0611/declare-your-own-financial-independence-day.aspx

PROLOGIS. (2021, March 9). *Forever altered: The further of logistics real estate demand.* Market Environment. https://www.prologis.com/news-research/global-insights/forever-altered-future-logistics-real-estate-demand

Razali, M. N., Adnan, Y. M., Jalil, R. A., & Esha, Z. (2021). Real estate investment trusts' (REITs) asset management strategies within real estate investment trusts (REITs). *Real Estate Management and Valuation, March.* https://doi.org/10.2478/remav-2021-0007

Reuters Staff. (2020, November 2). *Mall operator CBL files for Chapter 11 bankruptcy protection.* https://www.reuters.com/article/us-cbl-associates-bankruptcy-idUSKBN27I0UB

S&P DOW JONES INDICES. (2020, March 28). *Variations in REIT Sectors – Time to Go Defensive.* https://www.spglobal.com/en/research-insights/articles/variations-in-reit-sectors-time-to-go-defensive

Sismanis, N. (2022, September 30). *2 REITs with the World's Most Reliable Tenant.*

TipRanks. https://www.nasdaq.com/articles/2-reits-with-the-worlds-most-reli able-tenant

Summerhill Commercial. (2023, January 31). *Debunking common misconceptions about commercial real estate. https://www.summerhillcommercial.com/blog/debunking-common-misconceptions-about-c.* https://www.summerhillcommercial.com/blog/debunking-common-misconceptions-about-commercial-real-estate-investment/

Tarrant, H. (n.d.). Building blocks. JSE Magazine. https://www.jsemagazine.co.za/sector-focus/reits-sector-returns/

Tayf Egypt. (2023, August 14). *The Role of Sustainable Development in Commercial Real Estate Investment.* Linkedin. https://www.linkedin.com/pulse/roleof-sustainable-development-commercial-real-estate-investment

The Investopedia Team. (2022, April 6). *Beginner's Guide to Hedging: Definition and Example of Hedges in Finance.* Investopedia. https://www.investopedia.com/trading/hedging-beginners-guide/

The Law Library of Congress. (n.d.). *Real estate industry: A resource guide.* https://guides.loc.gov/real-estate-industry-sources/investment-trusts#:~

Thomas, N. (2023, July 2). *The importance of REITs in your investment portfolio.* Jamaica Observer. https://www.jamaicaobserver.com/style/the-importance-of-reits-in-your-investment-portfolio/

Uche, O. (2023, August 3). *The rise of proptech: How technology is revolutionizing real estate investing.* Linkedin. https://www.linkedin.com/pulse/rise-proptech-how-technology-revolutionizing-real-estate-onu-uche

Uhlig, H. (2008, May 1). *Mortgage-backed securities and the financial crisis of 2008: a post mortem.* Becker Friedman Institute. https://bfi.uchicago.edu/insight/research-summary/mortgage-backed-securities-and-the-financial-crisis-of-2008-a-post-mortem/

Wachtell, Lipton, Rosen, & Katz. (2020). Real estate and REIT *M&A.* https://www.wlrk.com/files/reit/WLRK.REMAcompil.pdf

IMAGE REFERENCES

Antranias. (2014, January 17). *Bridge web bridge piers pier.* [Image]. Pixabay. https://pixabay.com/photos/bridge-web-bridge-piers-pier-246913/.

Dhage, S. (2021, December 17). *A computer-generated image of a cube surrounded by smaller cubes.* [Image]. Unsplash. https://unsplash.com/photos/a-computer-generated-image-of-a-cube-surrounded-by-smaller-cubes-_rZnChsIFuQ?utm_content=credit ShareLink&utm_medium=referral&utm_source=unsplash.

Gorecki, J. (2017, August 14). *Gazoport gas cylinders Poland.* [Image]. Pixabay. https://pixabay.com/photos/gazoport-gas-cylinders-poland-2639720/.

Grabowska, K. (2020, May 12). *Ten dollars with inscription and building.* [Image]. Pexels. https://www.pexels.com/photo/ten-dollars-with-inscription-and-building-4386156/.

Housel, M. (2020, June 19). *Black and white crew neck shirt.* [Image]. Unsplash. https://

unsplash.com/photos/black-and-white-crew-neck-shirt-Xl-6WjqcppQ?utm_con
tent=creditShareLink&utm_medium=referral&utm_source=unsplash.

Koval, R. (2023, January 20). *Make mistakes mug.* [Image]. Pexels. https://www.pexels.com/photo/make-mistakes-mug-15223238/.

McBee, D. (2017, December 11). *Bitcoins and US dollar bills.* [Image]. Pexels. https://www.pexels.com/photo/bitcoins-and-u-s-dollar-bills-730547/.

McBee, D. (2018, October 28). *High angle shot of suburban neighborhood.* [Image]. Pexels. https://www.pexels.com/photo/high-angle-shot-of-suburban-neighborhood-1546168/.

Mils, A. (2019, March 28). *Fan of 100 US dollar banknotes.* [Image]. Unsplash. https://unsplash.com/photos/fan-of-100-us-dollar-banknotes-lCPhGxs7pww?utm_con
tent=creditShareLink&utm_medium=referral&utm_source=unsplash.

Nekrashevich, A. (2021, February 12). *Marketing businessman person hands.* [Image]. Pexels. https://www.pexels.com/photo/marketing-businessman-person-hands-6802049/.

Nilov, M. (2021, April 29). *Person's hand reaching out to a light.* [Image]. Pexels. https://www.pexels.com/photo/person-s-hand-reaching-out-to-a-light-7709020/.

Oleksandr, P. (2021, June 11). *Couple buying a new home.* [Image]. Pexels. https://www.pexels.com/photo/couple-buying-a-new-home-8292805/.

Parker, C. (2020, November 10). *Majestic stone building near glass skyscraper in downtown.* [Image]. Pexels. https://www.pexels.com/photo/majestic-stone-building-near-glass-skyscraper-in-downtown-5847573/.

Pixabay. (2016, December 24). *Architecture black and white challenge chance.* [Image]. Pixabay. https://www.pexels.com/photo/architecture-black-and-white-challenge-chance-277593/.

Shimazaki, S. (2020, October 22). *Judgement scale and gavel in judge office.* [Image]. Pexels. https://www.pexels.com/photo/judgement-scale-and-gavel-in-judge-office-5669602/.

Shute, A. (2021, September 25). *A scrabbled word spelling the word W is down on top of a.* [Image]. Unsplash. https://unsplash.com/photos/a-scrabbled-word-spelling-the-word-w-is-down-on-top-of-a-QnRDKNbKl9k?utm_content=creditShareLink&utm_medium=referral&utm_source=unsplash.

Sometimesfay. (2016, April 18). *New York WTC cityscape skyline.* [Image]. Pixabay. https://pixabay.com/photos/new-york-wtc-cityscape-skyline-1332374/.

Studio_Iris. (2023, March 28). *Podcast microphone music audio.* [Image]. Pixabay. https://pixabay.com/photos/podcast-microphone-music-audio-7876792/.

Winkler, M. (2023, September 25). *A typewriter with a paper that says resilience building.* [Image]. Pexels. https://www.pexels.com/photo/a-typewriter-with-a-paper-that-says-resilience-building-18500689/.

Yaqubov, R. (2023, July 20). *View of an oil rig near the shore.* [Image]. Pexels. https://www.pexels.com/photo/view-of-an-oil-rig-near-the-shore-17668423/.

www.ingramcontent.com/pod-product-compliance
Lightning Source LLC
Chambersburg PA
CBHW050501190326
41458CB00005B/1377